DISCARD

Life, Liberty

and the Pursuit of Happiness

Life, Liberty
and the Pursuit of Happiness

the memoirs of

Ralph J. Temple

Published by Akashic Books
©2011 by the Estate of Ralph J. Temple

ISBN-13: 978-1-61775-104-2
Library of Congress Control Number: 2011940041

Akashic Books
PO Box 1456
New York, NY 10009
info@akashicbooks.com
www.akashicbooks.com

Of the many persons I came to admire during my years with the ACLU, I put none ahead of Ralph. He personifies the virtues that the ACLU displays at its best: a fierce commitment to civil liberty; imagination, energy, skill, and industry; integrity; persuasiveness; and a fine blend of irascibility, good humor, and anger. Ralph is moderate but never mealy-mouthed; passionate but never hysterical; moral but never pious.
—Aryeh Neier,
Former Executive Director, ACLU

For a lot of people coming out of law school looking for public interest jobs, there are a relative handful of people in this country who are heroes, models to be followed, people who are known among young lawyers and who are admired for the example they set. I think Ralph deserves that reputation as much as anyone I know.
—Ira Glasser,
Former Executive Director, ACLU

It isn't just that Ralph has a passionate concern to see that civil liberties are protected. I have that and so do you. We all share a concern to guard our constitutional rights. But Ralph Temple has the knowledge and the skill to make this concern victorious.
—Hilda Howland M. Mason,
District of Columbia City Council

TABLE OF CONTENTS

Ralph J. Temple was born in England on October 18, 1932. Shortly before his father was called into the Royal British Army in 1940, Temple fled with his mother by boat from the Nazi attack on London and settled in Miami, Florida. He graduated from Miami Beach High School in 1951 and obtained a law degree from Harvard Law School in 1956.

He worked for Thurgood Marshall at the NAACP Legal Defense Fund from 1956–57, until being drafted into the United States Army. He taught law at Harvard, George Washington, and Howard universities before becoming an associate attorney at Arnold, Fortas & Porter in 1962.

A critical formative experience was Ralph's August 1964 trip to St. Augustine, Florida with the New York City Lawyers Constitutional Defense Fund while an associate at Arnold, Fortas & Porter; he spent two weeks there with Alvin Bronstein working to ensure compliance with the newly enacted 1964 Civil Rights Act. (Just two months earlier, Dr.

Martin Luther King Jr. had been arrested in St. Augustine for sitting in at a restaurant.)

When moving to the American Civil Liberties Union, Ralph soon found his calling as a civil rights and civil liberties attorney, rising to the position of Legal Director of the ACLU of the National Capital Area in Washington, D.C., where he served from 1966–80. In 2008, the D.C. ACLU presented him with their annual Alan and Adrienne Barth Award for Exemplary Volunteer Service.

He was married to Sally Brown from 1960–81 and had two children, Kathy and Johnny. In 1990, Ralph married Ann Macrory and in 1996 they moved from D.C. to Ashland, Oregon, where Ralph was active in local politics on behalf of the ACLU and successfully opposed the use of tasers by the police.

Ralph kept up his legal activism and civic organizing until the day he passed away on August 27, 2011. On September 18, 2011, he was recognized by the ACLU Foundation of Oregon for his brilliant and tireless work on behalf of civil liberties.

———————————

This volume comprises Ralph J. Temple's memoirs of his life and work. The majority of the stories and essays were written between 1998 and 2003, though also included are writings from before and after that period.

PART I

THE IMMIGRANT IN MIAMI

EARLY ENCOUNTERS WITH THE ALMIGHTY
1936

Hebrew school began when I was barely five years old, and over the next year or so I learned how to read Hebrew, and was introduced to Jewish history and ritual. At four or five, I even saw G-d, or at least thought I did. I was in shul with my father at the Shabbos service, and after a while I whispered to my father, "Where's G-d? Where's heaven?" My father, continuing to chant the liturgy, pointed upward, and I, misunderstanding, spotted and fixed in my mind the faces of two old men praying in the balcony. I can still see the narrow, pointed-chin face of Heaven, and the oval, kindly face of G-d.

G-d was, of course, exalted. So sanctified, in fact, that Jews have no corporeal embodiment of G-d, like Jesus or Krishna or Buddha; they don't even write His name. In the Judaic texts, the Hebrew characters, pronounced *Adonoy*, are only an abbreviation of G-d's name. The notion stuck; I still compulsively follow my parents' form of hyphenating the name in English. So the Lord was ineffable.

But He was also down-to-earth. My grandfather—my father's father—was an orthodox rabbi. I met him in late 1940, when I was eight years old and my mother and I had just come to America. During the few months we had around each other before he unexpectedly passed on, he was sweet and attentive. He kept a gentle but deliberate eye on my religion, and once, when we were standing side by side at a public urinal in Brooklyn, he taught me the Hebrew prayer thanking G-d for a good pee. G-d has ever since been the donor of all gifts, special and routine.

The connection really began, though, before my grandfather and before Hebrew school. Even at three or four, in bed before sleep, I knew that my protracted prayers, calling attention to each family member and friend, were directed to a Listener.

G-d was also the first to experience my capacity for anger, apparently inherited from my mother. More than once, I had a fit as I struggled haplessly with cardboard cut-out airplanes that were supposed to be folded, with tabbed inserts holding the shape and parts together. They wouldn't hold, and I knew Who was responsible for my torment. He was no abstraction to me; the relationship was very personal—one on One. Screaming, I would crumple and tear the planes, and, looking upward, unleash on the Almighty the full force of my limited repertoire of epithets.

Once I made the mistake of writing them down in a small notebook my parents had given me. There, carefully inscribed in my unmistakable handwriting, my parents discovered the sentences *G-d is a sod* and *G-d is a bleaten sod*. These were the worst—the only—bad words I knew. My parents sat down with me and gingerly approached the subject. When they showed me the sentences in the notebook, I was shocked. For the first time in my life, I lied, and claimed that I had not written those words and didn't know who had. The two of them said that G-d loved me and they knew that I loved Him, and that if anything ever really bothered me, to let them know, because they loved me too. And that was that. They let me off the hook.

I was thankful that G-d had imbued my parents with wisdom and compassion. So I let Him off the hook too.

EDGEWARE
1938

[Y]ou suddenly find your tongue twisted and your speech stammering as you seek to explain to your six-year-old daughter why she can't go to the public amusement park that has just been advertised on television, and see tears welling up in her little eyes . . .
        —Dr. Martin Luther King Jr.,
    "Letter From Birmingham Jail" (1963)

My moment of truth came when I was five years old and got called a Jew-name for the first time in my life.

We were the first Jewish family to move into the quiet residential neighborhood of Edgeware, Middlesex, a suburb in northwest London. My father, an up-and-coming certified public accountant, had moved us there in 1933, out of Stepney Green, the Jewish ghetto in the East End of London, where I had been born the year before.

Our new home in Edgeware, at 12 Cheyneys Avenue, was a modest redbrick, two-story duplex in a tidy little neighborhood. It had a small front yard with a green gate, and a rear garden looking across a five-foot fence to rolling hills and the tracks of London's commuter train lines. The trains going by regularly were not a disturbance. My father loved working in the garden, and made it beautiful.

The neighbors had welcomed us warmly. Cathy and George Parker, in the house next to ours, and Olive and George Avrill, two houses up, became life-long friends. Some fifty years later, in 1983, on one of our return visits, my mother and I made a special trip down to Brighton to spend a happy afternoon with the widows Cathy and Olive.

One of my playmates, however, had an anti-Semitic father, and one sunny afternoon, as we were playing in the street after school, Stephen called me a "cowardly Jew." It did not mean very much to me, and I took no particular offense. I sensed, though, that it was meaningful to Stephen, who delivered it with unusual zest.

In 1938, when this occurred, Adolph Hitler had been in power for five years. The Germans had marched into the Rhineland, and, emboldened by the Western powers' inertia and fear, proceeded on to other invasions. The persecution of Jews began in Germany, in 1933, with boycotts against Jewish shops and businesses, and humiliations and beatings in the streets. In 1935, the Nuremberg Laws were enacted, severely restricting Jews' civil rights, and barring them from major fields of employment. In March 1938, Hitler occupied Austria, sparking a mass exodus of Jews trying to escape from the escalating danger. Few conceived of the magnitude of the impending horror, the harnessing of modern industrial techniques—the assembly line and mass production—for the systematic extermination of the Jews of Europe.

My mother was a petite woman, just over five feet tall, at about one hundred pounds. She was gentle and compassionate, warm and cheerful. Except when defending hearth and home. Then, as in Kipling's *The Female of the Species*, an intruder

> . . . *will meet no cool discussion, but the instant, white-hot wild*
> *Wakened female of the species warring as for spouse and child.*

My mother's anger could get like that.

When I told her what Stephen had called me, my mother let out a loud scream, grabbed me by the arm, and hauled me out to the front of the house. Stephen was still there, about three houses away. Seeing my mother gesturing toward him as she spoke to me, Stephen sank down behind some hedges, trying to hide. My mother took hold of my small, five-year-old right hand and balled it up.

"See that?" she said. "That's a fist. Now go over there and hit Stephen with your fist. In the face. Tell him never again to call you a name about being Jewish."

"I don't want to," I whimpered.

My mother raised her hand as if about to slap me. "You go over there and hit him!" she shouted.

I walked over to where Stephen was crouching in the bushes, frightened and crying. He pleaded, "Please, Ralph, don't hit me, please." He looked wretched.

I really didn't want to hit him. The idea was not appealing. Besides, his face had gotten snotty with his blubbering.

"I'm sorry, Stephen," I said. "My mother says I have to hit you."

I punched him in the face with my fist. Not all that hard, not much more than a poke. But in the state he was in, it was enough. He howled.

"Don't call me names about being Jewish," I said.

Maybe no one sails through life under any one banner. But

surely, one of mine became that of the curled rattlesnake with the slogan *Don't Tread on Me*. Whether genes, karma, or my mother's lesson—I never again had to be reminded to strike back.

EXPLOSION
1940

The heart-shaking sound and the rumble of the floor and walls snap me bolt upright on the toilet. It's dawn. The passengers, startled out of sleep and still in night clothes, pour into the ship's narrow corridors, their panic somewhat restrained by stoic British coolness.

My mother won't be cool, though. She has awakened in a cabin missing a seven-year-old. I hope she knows I've only gone up the hall to the WC. My heart's pounding. I've got to get back to the cabin, back to her. I don't know what's happening, what we're supposed to do next. She'll know. The corridor is blocked by wall-to-wall chattering, bewildered people. I've got to get through; I've got to get back to her.

My mother had not wanted to leave England. She didn't want to leave her husband. She didn't want to leave her mother and father—or her grandmother, sisters, uncles, and aunts—her world. But it was September 1940, the German Blitzkrieg was underway, and for six weeks we had been sleeping in an air raid shelter, listening to antiaircraft shells and bombs exploding in the night.

Sometimes the German bombers got past the coast without being detected, and the first warning was not the siren, but explosions. One afternoon, when we were in the East End of London, I remember my mother, with me in her arms, running with many others in the streets amid the din of explosions, to the tunneled public shelter in Beaumont Street Park, a block from my grandparents' house. After the raid, it was strange to see houses sliced open and their insides exposed, the profiles of the different floors, the furniture, scattered clothing and belongings, piles of rubble. Once, we spent all night with neighbors and strangers in the Beaumont Street public shelter.

There were also nightly bombings in Edgeware, the northwest suburb where we lived. A raid caught us by surprise one night. As some of our windows shattered, my father herded my mother and me from our upstairs bedrooms down to the parlor, where he turned over a settee and two armchairs, pushed them together to form a cover, and, as we huddled under them, covered us with his body, his arms around us. I have no memory of fear, only of feeling safe and of loving my father. My father then had a brick shelter built in our garden, and, with raids getting us up every night, finally put in mattresses and made the shelter our bedroom.

Few British or European Jews were as lucky as we; few could escape. America, still staggering out of the Depression, was unwilling to risk a flood of refugees on the job market. It was no help that the man in charge of visas in President Roosevelt's State Department was Breckenridge Long, a South Carolina racist who adamantly opposed the admission of refugees—particularly Jews. Opinion polls showed that a majority of Americans felt the same way.

The greatest regret of Eleanor Roosevelt's life, according to historian Doris Kearns Goodwin, was her inability to persuade her husband to open America to Europe's per-

secuted Jews. The president, plagued with political problems in trying to get an isolationist Congress and country
to support Britain's defense effort, did not want to buck
the anti-immigrant, anti-Semitic tide. Then, as now, America could not live up to Emma Lazarus's magnanimous im-
age emblazoned on the Statue of Liberty:

> *Give me your tired, your poor,*
> *Your huddled masses yearning to breathe free,*
> *The wretched refuse of your teeming shore.*
> *Send these, the homeless, tempest-tost to me,*
> *I lift my lamp beside the golden door!*

In May 1939, the world endured the spectacle, similar
to refugee tragedies we see today, of the *St. Louis*, carrying
930 Jews from Germany, barred from docking in Havana.
For weeks the ship hovered close enough to Miami for the
refugees to see the city lights while negotiators tried fruit-
lessly to get the United States to let them in. A telegram
to President Roosevelt from a committee of the passengers
went unanswered. The *St. Louis* was forced to return to Europe, where many of its passengers died in concentration
camps.

We were among the few fortunate enough to be offered
sanctuary. My father's parents, having immigrated and become American citizens in the 1930s, offered to take us in
and provide for us for the duration of the war.

At first, my mother refused to leave. "We will all see it
through together," she told my father. "The whole family."

"We must get the child to safety," he insisted. "We
can't send him over alone; you must go with him."

His position was compelling. A German invasion of
England appeared an imminent possibility. My father, a

thirty-five-year-old accountant, was to be drafted into the British army, and the rest of the family would soon be forced by the bombings to leave their London homes for refuge in the Midlands. My mother relented.

It was a dangerous time to cross the Atlantic, which was swarming with German submarines. My father later described the torment of his decision to send us away, in the first letter he wrote following our departure, on September 24, 1940, perhaps the same day I was struggling to get back to my mother in the aftermath of the explosion:

> *Day and night I searched deeply within my heart for the answer: should I send you or not. That answer I never found completely. I knew only that I loved you two little souls with every fibre of my being. So I chose what seemed to be the lesser of two risks, both fraught with danger, and threw myself, in utter faith upon our Creator.*

I can see him in the small room in Liverpool, where the three of us stayed the night before my mother and I embarked. It is morning, and he stands at the room's small sink in his white shorts, shaving. When we went to breakfast, my parents were in for another jolt when they saw the headlines: *Refugee Ship "City of Benares" Hit By U-boats—Goes Down With 1,500.*

"We'll go back," my father said to my mother. "You don't have to go. We'll go home."

"No," said my mother. "We'll go." My mother shared my father's conviction that G-d would carry us across safely.

The *Samaria* was built, along with two other steamships, the *Scythia* and the *Laconia*, as Cunard Line luxury ocean liners, in Birkenhead in 1920. They were modest in size compared with the great ocean liners, but had classic lines and palatial elegance. The *Samaria* was 624 feet long and could carry 1,800 passengers. She was built with a black hull, a giant red smokestack, gleaming white deck structures, a writing room, a smoking room, a bar, a garden lounge, a dining room, and a gymnasium. In 1940, she and her sister ships were drafted into the war, stripped down, painted a less conspicuous gray, and equipped with canons and antisubmarine depth charges. The *Scythia* saw action as a troop ship. The *Laconia* was torpedoed off the coast of West Africa, only a hundred of the 2,700 on board surviving. Our ship, the *Samaria*, made it through the war as a refugee ship, and then enjoyed a return to civilian life, until it was scrapped in 1956.

On October 6, 1940, in my father's second letter to us in America, he wrote:

> *When I left you I watched the river all day, and passed your ship (I soon ascertained that it was the "Samaria") in the ferry boats several times, waving at figures I could not distinguish hoping you could recognize me by my uniform.*

He told of attempting to get on the ship for one last goodbye:

> *I tried every known Authority on shore in the vain hope of getting a Permit admitting me on board ship or even on the dockside—it didn't work. After some hours I knew you were going to make the trip, and I appreciate what courage it needed to go through with it, dearest.*

Then he described seeing us go:

> *About four p.m., at high tide, I watched the tugs nosing your*

ship around in mid-stream and saw the destroyer (small but pleasant sight) at your side . . . I took a last look, not in sadness but rather in hope, and made my way home.

He braced my mother and himself for the hard times ahead by hoping for a happier future:

Great and terrible things are taking place, happenings that are breaking & shaking whole lives. Let us both conduct ourselves responsibly and determine that when the happy day of reunion arrives we shall both be ready for a life of ecstasy that will re-pay us for every moment of suffering and loneliness.

But for a brief interlude in 1946, it would be ten years before we would be together again.

The explosion still reverberates as I ply through the mass of people. I turn and twist down the corridor, under, around, and between legs. My mother, hysterical, is carving a path through the crowd toward me. I fly into her arms, which wrap around me, and feel her wet kisses and warm tears.

I am safe.

Announcements are made and the ship's stewards circulate the good news. We are not hit. The explosion was a depth charge fired defensively at a pursuing U-boat. For most of the ten-day crossing we are in convoy, sometimes with war ships, sometimes escorted by planes. There are no other incidents.

"Explosion," from the Latin *explodere*, driven away. Driven away from country, from family, from home. But safe. The Statue of Liberty, the promised land, are only days away.

LIFE AT 542 JEFFERSON
1943

The Army Air Force occupied Miami Beach during World War II, and turned all the hotels into barracks. Squads of soldiers marched through the streets, and, with the corporal or sergeant in charge calling out the chorus, sang songs like:

Oh, oh, oh . . . oh li'l Liza, little Liza Dee,
Oh, oh, oh . . . oh li'l Liza, little Liza Dee . . .

And:

I've got sixpence, jolly, jolly sixpence,
I've got sixpence, to last me all my life:
I've got two pence to spend, and two pence to lend
And two pence to send home to my wife, dear wife . . .

My mother and I, as refugees from the Nazi Blitzkrieg of London, were separated from my father who, at a ripe thirty-eight, was being drafted into the British Army. We made ourselves a snug nest of our humble apartment at 542 Jefferson Avenue on Miami Beach.

We moved into Apartment 8 in 1942, when I was nine years old, and stayed there until 1950, when I was seventeen and my father rejoined us and moved us to a roomier, more upscale place. In the 1940s and 1950s, those who were well-off lived from 6th Street to 10th or 11th. Those who were lush lived north of 11th Street, and the neighborhoods of the not-so-well-off to the poor stretched from our place down to Biscayne, the southernmost street on Miami Beach, where my friend Red Heller lived in a small shacklike house.

Our apartment was the last one on the ground floor of the building, on the left side of the dimly lit, long hallway, and looked out on an alley, which was my principal stamping grounds in my preteen and early teen years. The living room of our apartment, about twenty feet by twenty feet, converted into our bedroom at night, by pulling my Murphy bed out of a closet, while my mother slept on the sofa. From the living room, a door opened to a small dining-kitchen area, and another door from that into a tiny dressing room–bathroom area.

I had enough adventures in that little place—from intruders coming through the windows from the alley, to getting caught smoking, to not getting caught in my first awkward fumblings with a girl—to fill a book.

The girl caper was a joint venture of Marvin Sager and me, when we were fourteen. While my mother was at work, we got the neighborhood tomboy, Ginger, who was ten and one of the neighborhood gang who played and hung around in my alley, to join us in that tiny dressing room–bathroom area for an exchange of viewing of private parts. I got about six inches away from Ginger's part, because I'd only once before seen one, and that was eleven years earlier when I was only three and Annie, the three-and-a-half-year-old from next door, had exchanged looks with me. Ginger was hairless and her part seemed to be only a slit, but I snuck a sniff, and found her altogether satisfying. We finished our looking, then hustled to get out of there so as not to get caught.

After that, Ginger started to follow me around everywhere in the neighborhood. "Go away," I said, "stop being a pest." She'd just smile and continue to follow me. I'd wake up weekend mornings, and she'd be sitting on the windowsill outside our apartment, staring at me and waiting for me to wake up. "Ginger's really gotten attached to you, hasn't she?" asked my puzzled mother. "Oh, she's just a pest," I said.

One day after Ginger and I had had a fight about something, she retaliated by dipping one of my kittens, which were in a box under the rear outside stairs of my apartment building, into a bucket of water. I sought Ginger out, chased her across an empty lot, and whacked her on the rear with a handful of weeds we called "sticker," causing her to wail in pain. A short time later, she showed up with a smaller friend, standing outside our alley window and calling, "Ralph's Mother, Ralph's Mother!"

"Go away," I said to her from inside the apartment.

"Who is that, what's going on?" my mother asked, coming over to the window.

"Its just that pest Ginger," I said. "Pay no attention to her, Mum."

"What is it, Ginger?" my mother asked.

"Ralph chased me, and whacked me with stickers, and really hurt me," whined Ginger.

"Ralph!" said my mother. "Why would you do such a thing?"

"Because she stuck one of my kittens in water and got it all wet," I said answered.

"Ginger," demanded my inspector-general mother, "that's an awful thing to do."

At this point, Ginger's little girl friend piped up for the first time: "You know what else he did to Ginger?"

Ginger, dismayed, hissed at her friend, "No, sshhh," then grabbed her by the hand and they both ran off.

My mother just shook her head. "Don't be mean to her," she said. And that was that. Whew!

The bottom line is that 542 Jefferson Avenue was a safe, happy place for me. I was a single-parent, latchkey child, as my mother worked six days a week in Miami, across the bay from Miami Beach. It did not mean neglect to me; it meant freedom.

When there were crises, it turned out that I lived in the village that Hillary Clinton says it takes to raise a child. Once, when I was twelve, I gashed my knee, and ran to Greenbaum's, the neighborhood grocery store. Pete Kaplan, the soft-drink and candy concessionaire, phoned his wife to come from their apartment across the street and cover for him while he drove me in his pickup truck to a doctor on Lincoln Road, who closed the wound with nine stitches. A similar thing happened when I accidentally took a nail through one of my fingers.

Some scars carry good memories.

SCHOOL DAY MEMORIES
1944

My daughter Kathy is a public school teacher in Tucson and tells me that a teacher has to be cautious even about taking an unruly child by the arm. Teachers had more leeway in my school days.

In the second grade I attended Orange Glade Elementary School in Miami, run by a principal named Miss Cornelius. One lunchtime I was sitting in Corny's office by her desk while writing five hundred times, *I will not disturb those around me with my constant chatter,* when Miss Dillard, our second grade teacher, hauled my classmate Adrienne into the office. Miss Dillard held Adrienne by the elbow so that the child's small frame was stretched and tipped over. It was sad to see the normally cheerful and peppy Adrienne keelhauled in this manner. Miss Dillard indignantly reported that Adrienne had used a dirty word and leaned over to whisper to Miss Cornelius the offending phrase, which I was close enough to hear: "Son of a bitch." Corny looked sternly at Adrienne and told her she mustn't use that kind of language, that people would think her parents spoke that way. To which Adrienne straightforwardly replied that her daddy said that all the time. Miss Cornelius and Miss Dillard exchanged a glance, and Miss Cornelius then ordered the miscreant taken to the restroom and her mouth washed out with soap. Five minutes later they returned, with Adrienne looking the unhappiest I'd ever seen her, frothy bubbles oozing from her tightly closed lips. At Miss Dillard's direction, Adrienne opened wide, displaying a mouthful of suds. No wonder the kids called the place the "Four C" school—"Corny's Corny Concentration Camp."

Once, after Miss Dillard caught Jack and me fighting during recess, she berated us in front of the class, and since this was the spring of 1941—I was newly arrived, and the United States had not yet entered World War II—she concluded her admonition by saying, "Ralph, you've come here from Europe where there is a war, but in America we are peaceful, so you must learn not to fight"—just in case I didn't already feel somewhat dislocated.

Another time Miss Dillard took the class on a visit to the Miami City Hall, where we chatted with various officials, each child getting to sit in the chair of the official whose role he or she had assumed. Our visit included the city jail on the top floor of the ten-story building, and we looked with wonder at the bedraggled unfortunates behind bars. One of them, a young woman—either a drunk or a prostitute—greeted us with a warm smile, and said, "Ain't it nice, y'all are in skoll. I was a skoll teacher oncet." When we were back in class reviewing our field trip, Miss Dillard made fun of the prisoner, mimicking her, "*I was a skoll teacher oncet.*" Miss Dillard was not my favorite.

South Beach Elementary School, which I attended from third through sixth grade after we moved to Miami Beach, proved even more harsh in some respects. I don't mean Miss Patton, our fourth grade teacher, who liked children and was kind—even though she once grabbed me by my long curly hair and shook me till my teeth rattled. And I don't mean Miss Carr, our tall, skinny, and ancient sixth grade teacher who would abruptly rap us with a ruler on the arm, knuckles, or head. I mean Mr. Frizzan, who once grabbed me in a hallway, clasped my head between his knees, and pounded me on the backside with a hefty encyclopedia.

Even worse was Miss Singletary, South Beach's tall and strong disciplinary teacher. Each day, when the lunch period ended, the classes formed lines in front of the building to listen to announcements. Patrol boys wearing silver badges pinned to white-striped belts across their chests monitored the lines, plucking out those who talked or were otherwise disorderly. After classes resumed, those selected had to line up outside Miss Singletary's classroom and bend over a chair, where they were paddled on the backside by Miss Singletary, wielding a board in which air holes served to increase the force and thus the pain.

I always kept quiet in the after-lunch line because I feared Miss Singletary, a sort of Mrs. Pruneface out of the Dick Tracy comics. But, like the ill-fated main character in John O'Hara's *Appointment in Samara*, I was doomed to have an encounter with my nemesis. One day in the sixth grade, when Miss Carr was out sick and there was no substitute quickly available, we were asked to study quietly until one could be rounded up. I could not resist the opportunity, with the class unsupervised, to grab a handful of chalkboard erasers and start hurling them across the room at my pals. They took cover behind desks, grabbed erasers of their own, and threw a barrage back at me. I bided my time, waited until they were out of ammunition, then jumped up and unleashed a series of well-aimed potshots. Full of glee, shouting loudly, and not realizing why my friends were slowly rising from behind their barricades, I kept peppering them with shots, and only became aware that Miss Singletary had entered the room behind me when she spun me around by the shoulder, slapped me across the face, and yelled, "Didn't you hear me telling you to stop?" Startled and frightened, I sputtered, "No ma'am," only to get another slap with the back of her returning hand, and then a series of punches on my rear as she bent me over her upraised knee.

The most brutal, though, was the principal of South Beach, Mr. Saunders. In the fifth grade, Mr. Saunders once slapped my friend Neil in the face so hard that his ring left an impression on Neil's face that lasted all day. Another time, he whipped me on the backside with a leather strap in front of the class. The worst thing he did was to Barnett Sandler. Barnett was a troubled child who lived with his mother in the Smith Cottages, the only public housing project on 1940s Miami Beach. He had bad teeth, bad breath, bad grades, and was unruly and disliked by the other kids. Poor Barnett was a mess, and his mother did not know what to do with him. But Mr. Saunders did. The deed was performed in the hallway outside our classroom, with no witnesses at first except the participants. But I was sitting in the back row near the door, so when we were all frozen by the thumping on the wall, I peeked into the hallway and saw Barnett's mother standing there and her kid wailing in pain, while Mr. Saunders gripped his head and banged it against the wall.

In those days parents did not think to challenge the authority of school officials. That is, most parents. Ada Marcus, mother of my friend Jerry, was warm, loving, funny, and could be loud and crude. The Marcuses were in a rough business—Jerry's uncle, Al Goldman, owned several liquor stores in the "colored" section of Miami, and Jerry's father, Joe, managed them. It was a cash business which required having some muscle around to deter robbers—not uniformed security guards, but big, tough, mean-looking guys.

Some time after Jerry and I had left South Beach and gone on to a junior high school, good old Mr. Saunders whacked Jerry's kid brother Robby. Ada showed up at school the next day quite irate. Mr. Saunders responded by walking around his desk, closing the door to his office, then asking Ada to please calm down and have a seat. He pulled up a chair alongside her and said very quietly, "Mrs. Marcus, I appreciate your concern, but, you know, running a school is a difficult job. I am responsible for the education of these children and for maintaining an atmosphere in which they can learn. It is not easy. But you don't have to worry about it because it is my responsibility, not yours. And it is I, and not you, who will decide whether a child in the school needs to be disciplined, and what that discipline should be. And if I decide on corporal punishment," he concluded, leaning his face close to Ada's, "that is what will be done. Now, do you understand that?"

"Yeah?" Ada replied. "Lemme tell you somethin'—you lay a hand on my kid again and my husband Joe's gonna send some of his boys around to take care of you—you know what I mean?"

Robby never got hit again. I loved Ada Marcus.

A RALPH BY ANY OTHER NAME
1946

"Ralph" is not a name I would have picked. Its currency in our society is that of a doofus. Jackie Gleason's fat, hapless, and blustering bus driver was Ralph Cramden. In *Bananas*, when Woody Allen tries to sneak-buy a porno magazine in a drugstore, handing it to the cashier sandwiched between *Time* and *Newsweek*, the cashier shouts to another employee, "Hey, Ralph, this guy is buying *Wild Orgasms*—how much is it?"

No. I would have been Jeff. Jeff Kent. In fact, I *was* Jeff Kent. When I was a kid, I could not stand unfair and unhappy endings. So I would fantasize changing them.

Only much later did I discover that I was not alone in this. In an early James Michener novel about a writer, *The Fires of Spring*, the ten-year-old David—hearing his teacher read the class the end of the *Iliad*, where the Greeks sneak into Troy in their great wooden horse, murder the noble Hector, and sack the city—runs from the classroom screaming, "It's a lie!" That night, by candlelight in his small room in the county poor house, David rewrites the end of the *Iliad*, concluding with the lines:

And Hector lit a fire beneath the horse,
And burned up every Greek.

As Jeff Kent, I went further than that: I entered the stories myself. Jeff spent a lot of time behind enemy lines in World War II, rescuing brave spies and others who Ralph felt strongly about.

In the 1946 movie *For Whom the Bell Tolls*, the twenty-year-old Ingrid Bergman is pulled away on her horse screaming, "Roberto! Roberto!" as Gary Cooper, leg broken, is left behind in a mountain pass to die heroically machine-gunning Spanish fascists while the loyalist guerrillas escape.

I, the fourteen-year-old Jeff Kent, swooped in, pulled Roberto—Gary Cooper—up on my horse and got him the hell out of there. I had a more selfish alternative fantasy where I left Gary Cooper where he was, joined the escaping group, and comforted the heartbroken Maria—Ingrid Bergman—who then fell in love and slept with . . . *me*.

I have never stopped collecting endings I want to change. I want to enter James Jones's 1951 classic *From Here to Eternity* on Pearl Harbor Day 1941, get Private Robert E. Lee Prewitt off that Honolulu beach and back to his army unit, and make sure he comes through the war intact and ends up marrying the whore Lorene.

I want to bust Cool Hand Luke out of that chain-gang prison, snatch Jack Nicholson out of the cuckoo's nest before they lobotomize him, and plunge into the French Quarter of 1940s New Orleans, beat the crap out of Stanley Kowalski, and see that Blanche Dubois gets hitched up with Mitch.

Ralph's song is "to right every wrong" from the Don Quixote number "To Dream the Impossible Dream." No surprise that he started out as a movie usher and later became a lawyer for the American Civil Liberties Union.

SNOW WHITE AND THE SEVEN DWARVES AT MIAMI BEACH HIGH

—OR—

The Trouble with Republicans

1950

I was signing up for the fiftieth reunion of my high school class when I came to a question on the form calling for my best memory of high school. That called to mind the only time I was ever charged with a sex-related offense. It was all a misunderstanding. It happened during our senior year, and seven of us were hauled, not into court, but into the office of the principal. One of our teachers accused us of conducting an obscene sexual discourse in her class. The time was 1950, and the class was the first in Dade County, Florida—probably one of the first in the country—to take a cautious experimental step into the realm of high school sex education. At least, that was the original idea.

The class was assigned to Miss Birdie McAllister, ostensibly because she was the biology teacher. Miss McAllister was a tall and genteel Southern lady. Her straight spine bespoke her dignity and her rigidity. Birdie's face was birdlike, chinless, and stern. At forty-nine, Miss McAllister still lived at home with her mother, and, we were all convinced, was still a virgin. In short, it was the consensus that Miss McAllister got the course as a political compromise: she was the most sexless sentient being in the school, plant life included.

The courage it required of Miss McAllister to take on a classful of teenagers in such a setting never occurred to us at the time. She was a strong character, though, and she held all the cards.

Miami Beach in 1950 was a pretty sedate community. There were no such things as drugs or weapons. Although the school ranged the economic spectrum, from kids in public housing to the working poor, like me, to the children of rich hotel owners, it was homogeneously Jewish for ninety percent of the student body, and similarly Christian for ninety-nine percent of the faculty. There was no apparent religious tension between teachers and kids. This was before the American Civil Liberties Union went to court and got G-d expelled from public schools, so we mediated the theological divide with the daily recitation of the Lord's Prayer and a joint annual Christmas-Hanukkah program.

The only time I can remember religion becoming an issue, it worked in my favor. In the eighth grade, a huge kid named Mel Minninson had playfully swatted me in the belly, knocking the wind out of me. Passing him an hour later in the hallway, I hurled myself at him, pounding his chest, about as far up as I could reach. Mel, or "Chinky" as he was called due to an Asian aspect in his Jewish face, seized and raised me in outstretched arms over his head, preparing to throw me to the ground, when Miss Spence, a teacher, came upon the scene.

"Melvin Minninson!" she screamed. "What's the matter with you? Put that boy down this minute! Do you hear me?" Poor Melvin, feeling misused, blurted out, "Jesus Christ!"

He had, of course, blundered onto sensitive ground.

Miss Spence, oblivious to any other circumstance, marched him off to the dean's office to answer for profaning the name of the Lord. It was one of my better scores against Chinky.

The students were also culturally separated from the mostly Southern teachers by the fact that many of us were transplants from New York and other points north.

None of which daunted Miss McAllister. She was up to the challenge of supressing any sexual intimations that might threaten to corrupt this early experiment in sex education. First, she named the course "Effective Living," thus broadening its conception. Next, she led the class in developing the outline of subjects and schedule for the semester, so cleverly directing the process that, by the time it was done, the course resembled a sort of hybrid home economics–biology class, all but barren of sex. That whole subject was crowded into one small portion to which a single class session was allotted.

After that we had no thought of outwitting Miss McAllister. She ran a tight ship, and besides, we were heading toward graduation, scheduled for January 25, 1951, and our minds were on the future.

As fate would have it, about two-thirds of the way through the semester, when the sex day finally arrived, Miss McAllister was out sick. The substitute teacher asked us for the day's agenda, and the class happily obliged by pitching right into the subject. In truth, the discussion was quite tame, in keeping with the neo-Victorian age of the 1950s. We talked about dating, kissing, and French kissing, and tiptoed into petting and whether and when you ever should. The substitute, somewhat bewildered, told us after the class that she was impressed with our intelligence and maturity.

Maybe she was. Maybe that was the way she reported it to Miss McAllister. If she did, that's not the way Miss

McAllister heard it. The first word we got was a summons to each of the seven of us, the next day, to report to the principal's office.

The seven, the accused ringleaders of the illicit discussion, were Barton Goldberg, the president of our senior class; Phil Benzil, the vice president; Neil Useden and me, the cochairs of the Senior Class Day program; Eddie Jacobi, a natural-born leader; Irving "Red" Heller, a member of the school's prized football team; and one girl, Barbara Leonard, the boldest and the brightest.

When we arrived at his office, we found the principal, Olin C. Webb, sitting behind his desk. Irvin Katz, dean of boys, and Margaret Tarrer, dean of girls, sat side by side to the right of the desk, and Miss Catherine Moore, our homeroom teacher, and Miss McAllister, our accuser, sat on the left. All were quite grim-faced.

Mr. Webb beckoned us to take our places in an array of seven chairs facing his desk and arching between the two pairs of faculty members.

Without pausing for amenities, he addressed us: "You have been called here because Miss McAllister reports that yesterday, instead of conducting yourselves like the responsible adults we all have trusted you to be, you violated that trust, took advantage of Miss McAllister's absence and of the substitute teacher, and engaged in an irresponsible and indecent discussion." Pausing to scan our faces, Mr. Webb continued, "Now, we all know you well, and will not jump to any conclusions. But we want you to hear what Miss McAllister has to say. We will then give each of you an opportunity to account for your conduct."

Miss McAllister spoke next. She was upset and hurt. She was also furious. Her almost nonexistent chin was tucked further into her throat than usual, and she spoke with intensity.

"The substitute teacher reported to me that the class said you were supposed to talk about sex, and that you talked about sex between boys and girls very directly in a way that was foul and dirty. She said that you did this as if it were normal to have this kind of discussion in our school and in my class. She said that those who spoke did so without embarrassment and even with a sense of self-satisfaction."

Uh-oh, I thought, *she's right about the self-satisfaction.*

"The substitute identified each of you as the instigators of this obscene episode," Miss McAllister continued. "She was appalled. I feel that you took advantage of me, and that your conduct was a humiliation to me and to the school."

There followed a brief and deadly silence.

"Well," said Mr. Webb, "I believe those are some pretty serious charges, and I think you students owe Miss McAllister and the rest of us an explanation."

There was some comfort in the number of us accused. At seven, we constituted almost twelve percent of the sixty-member senior class. And they could not very well expel the whole class leadership in one fell swoop . . . could they? Just how much were they going to make us suffer for this? Might it affect our graduation, our chances of getting into college?

Each of us spoke about a minute or two. Our manner was subdued, but certain, Though unplanned, we all said pretty much the same thing. We said we did not think that anyone had done anything wrong. The topic of sex had been scheduled for that day, we said, and the discussion went into some detail, but nothing that could be called off-color. We felt the discussion had been appropriate. We were surprised to hear that the substitute teacher had disapproved, we said, because she told us that she thought it was a mature discussion.

Given the differences in our personalities and choice of

words, and the quality of respect and humility which all of us knew the occasion demanded, it was a good showing for the defense. It was left to our homeroom teacher, Miss Moore, however, to show us a class-act summation.

Catherine Moore was an extraordinary piece of work.

Half of us had not known her prior to this last semester of our senior year. We had been in a separate homeroom class. But the two thirty-member classes had been merged into a single homeroom for the last semester. From a distance, Miss Moore had seemed to my pal Phil Benzil and me to be a terror. She would spot us in school assemblies and glare at us until she drove the whispering or snickering out of us. She looked like a martinet, and we were at first dismayed to learn that our section was being joined with hers. As it turned out, she *was* a martinet—a strict disciplinarian. She was also a wise and deeply caring teacher who, in ways plain and subtle, took our teenage fire and the rampant energy and individuality of each of the sixty of us, and inspired and molded us into a single, striving, interrelated group. Never before had we so powerfully experienced commitment, not just to family, clique, or team, but to community. It was a profound parting lesson.

It was also a romance. By the time we seven found ourselves on the carpet before the principal, the whole class had fallen in love with Miss Moore. And she with us.

"Miss McAllister has been my colleague for some years," Miss Moore began, "and I know her to be a fine teacher. But I also know these students. I know every one of them. There has to have been a misunderstanding, because they would not have done anything indecent. They are as upright, as fine, and as splendid a group of young people as one could hope for, and I would stake my life on any one of them.

Miss Moore, usually so strong, so stolid, finished her

impassioned statement choking with emotion as tears streamed down her face.

The seven of us were stunned, and deeply moved, by what she said. I felt a lot more secure at this point, but also a lot more sober about what we had triggered.

Mr. Webb waited a minute or two, then asked Dean Katz and Dean Tarrer if they had anything to add. They both stated briefly and simply that they knew us to be good people.

Mr. Webb then thanked the faculty members for their contributions. He said he was glad we had the chance to discuss this matter thoroughly, and that we should all feel particularly grateful to Miss McAllister for being astute and caring enough to raise it. He said he believed this meeting had served to clear the air, and he was sure that each of us students would take to heart all of the things said here today, particularly the values stressed by Miss McAllister.

Mr. Webb then said he would like to talk to the men alone, and would greatly appreciate it if the ladies would give him that opportunity.

The three women faculty members and Barbara Leonard then exited, leaving us six boys with Principal Webb and Dean Katz.

Mr. Webb rose from behind his desk. Tall, with an oval face behind large glasses, he was a pleasant and cheerful man, rarely as stern as he'd seemed today.

"You bunch of long-legged goofs," he began. "As Miss Moore so eloquently put it, you are a fine group of people. But, contrary to what you think, you do not know it all. Not by a long shot. You've got a lot to learn."

Uh-oh, I thought, *where is this going?*

"Here you are," Mr. Webb continued, "all full of vim and vinegar, swelling with your new-felt powers of mind and body. Just waiting to march out into the world and conquer it. Which I have no doubt you will."

He scanned our faces, looking each of us in the eye, without rancor.

"Well, think about it then," he said. "You can figure it out. You may think that Miss McAllister is old-fashioned, behind the times, backwards. Miss McAllister is from a different generation than all of you. She came up in another time with other sensibilities. We all come up different. We don't have the same feelings. We're all individuals. She's had her own life's experiences, and they're not the same as yours."

Mr. Webb paused to let it sink in.

"Why not be compassionate and show the same respect for Miss McAllister's sensitivities that you would want shown for yours?" he asked. "That's what it's all about in the end, anyway—how tolerant, how considerate, how kind we all are to one another. I hope you will learn from this, not how good it is to be as right as you think you are, but how important it is to show compassion for others—to allow everyone to be the way he is."

In the years that followed, I lost track of the faculty members. All, that is, except Dean Katz. Irvin Katz was only twenty-eight at the time of the episode in Principal Webb's office, although I didn't think of him as young. Mr. Katz had been my English teacher in the eight grade, and he gently challenged us, assigning, among other readings, *Moby Dick*. He had taken a shine to me and was one of my early mentors.

What seemed lifetimes after we graduated, Mr. Katz got into trouble when a woman with whom he was living was charged with embezzling school funds, and Mr. Katz got caught up in the net, so that he, too, was indicted and prosecuted. Long gone from Florida, I found out about it from Red Heller, who had become a cop. Mr. Katz was acquitted by the jury. In February 1963, I wrote him from my law office in Washington, D.C., that I was relieved by his acquittal but sorry that he had been unjustly accused. I wrote that he had been an inspiring teacher and a good friend, and that his contributions would always mean the world to me. Twenty-three years later, in 1986, when I ran into him at our thirty-fifth class reunion, Mr. Katz introduced me to his wife and told her how I had written him an encouraging letter in an hour of need.

As for the seven of us, we all did well. Barton Goldberg became a respected banker, and Neil Useden made a fortune with creative construction of pension and insurance programs. Phil Benzil, a dentist and civic leader in his own town, became president of the Board of Education in the state of Maryland. Red Heller rose through the ranks to become second in command of the largest police department in Florida. When his marriage was ending in the 1970s, over twenty years after we graduated from high school, he looked up Barbara Leonard, his long-lost high school sweetheart, who had become a school teacher in New York; they are preparing to celebrate their twenty-fifth wedding anniversary.

I taught law at Harvard, Howard, and George Washington universities, practiced law, and became a lawyer for the American Civil Liberties Union.

The only one who arguably turned out bad was Eddie Jacobi. We saw each other for the first time after high school, at age fifty-three in 1986, at the thirty-fifth class reunion. Eddie, an executive with IBM, was as handsome and charming as ever. But he was a Republican in Atlanta. As we reminisced, I reminded him of the Great Birdie McAllister Sex Prosecution case.

"You know, Ed," I said, "that little talk by Olin C. Webb is something I've never forgotten. What a great lesson."

"Really?" he said quizzically. "Was that your take on it?"

"Sure," I said. "Wasn't it yours?"

"Aw, c'mon, Ralph," said Eddie. "It was a bum rap, and they all knew it. We kicked old Birdie's butt."

See, that's the problem I have with Republicans. They're all practicality. Not enough heart.

FRIENDS
1958

"**W**hat the hell is the matter with you?" I bellowed.

Red had just told us that when he was a rookie cop in Miami in the late 1950s, he'd had an off-duty job as a uniformed security guard at Funland. He said that his duties included telling African-Americans showing up with their children at the gate that colored people were not allowed in Funland.

I couldn't stand it and I was making a scene. It was mid-February 2001, and the two couples and I were in Mike Gordon's Seafood Restaurant on the 79th Street Causeway in Miami Beach. We were having one of the annual get-togethers that we'd been having for decades. Irving "Red" Heller, his wife Barbara Leonard, and I had been high school classmates. Red and I go back to 1942, the third grade. It was only seven years earlier that I had joined in comforting Red and Barbara as she fought and beat a brain cancer. And it was only two years earlier that Red and the other man with us at dinner, Phil Benzil, had supported me as I fought my way through a throat cancer. Phil and I go all the way back to the tenth grade in 1948. In 1955, I was best man at his and Naomi's wedding, and in 1960, he was best man at my first marriage.

Old friends.

Red had been talking about his upcoming retirement event, to honor him after forty-three years of public service, in which he'd risen to the rank of assistant director— number two on one of the largest police departments in the country, the 5,000-member Miami-Dade Public Safety Department. He'd spoken of a rewarding career, and how happy he was to count a number of black officials and staff among his closest friends in the department. He'd said it was a far cry from the racism of the 1950s when he began, and then confessed his participation in turning black families away from a public amusement park.

"How could you have done a thing like that?" I demanded.

"For G-d's sake," Red said, "lay off. I'm not proud of it. I was saying I was sorry about it."

"That's not enough," I pressed. "It's not enough just to say you're sorry. How could you do a thing like that to people in the first place? How could you turn away families, with their children? It's a flaw in your character."

Phil intervened: "C'mon, Ralph, he's saying he regrets it. Take it easy . . . Although I admit you've got a point; it's sickening that it happened at all."

"Why are you beating up on me like this over something that happened more than forty years ago?" asked Red.

"Because it never should have happened," I said. "It's not enough to say that segregation was the law, or that it was the universal custom in the South, or that you needed the extra money. A bell should have gone off in your head. A warning signal should've gone off, telling you that this is too much, that you can't do something like this—not for law, not for custom, not for money, not for anything. You lack an element of conscience."

Red had had enough. "Damn it!" he said, getting to his

feet. "Then if I'm so terrible and awful, you shouldn't be eating dinner with me. I'm getting out of here."

Phil was talking the whole time, trying to cool the situation, and Barbara and Naomi reacted by telling us both to calm down.

"No, don't do that," I said. "Don't leave."

"Why not?" said Red. "You're saying we're not friends anymore, so what's the point?"

"I'm not saying we're not friends anymore."

"Well, then what *are* you saying? I've got a flawed character. I'm unworthy. What the hell are you saying? I mean, do you love me or not?"

"Yes, I love you. I just can't stand the thought of it, that's all. I know you're a good human being. I know that was forty years ago and that you've done many good things. I respect you. Of course I love you. We'll be friends for life."

The storm was over. We all settled back into our dinner.

Red and I were on the phone the next day. We always rehash our get-togethers—the rehashing is as good as the times themselves. And we revisited issues we've covered many times in the years before.

I haven't always been the one to erupt in anger. Sometimes it's been Red when he thinks I've taken some position particularly crazy or insensitive to public safety or to the struggles and suffering of the police. Sometimes we even argue without anger.

Then there are the times when we just taunt each other. At the fiftieth reunion of our high school graduating class in Miami Beach, in April 2001, a classmate, June Zimmerman, got on my back about my opposition to the death penalty. She kept demanding to know what possible reason I could have to want to keep Timothy McVeigh, the

Oklahoma Federal Building bomber, alive. I don't have much patience for that level of analysis, and responded with questions like, "Why inject him—why not slice him up a sliver at a time, beginning with his testicles and keep him alive and screaming as long as possible?"

She complained to Red about what she viewed as the unresponsiveness of my arguments. He finally decided to join her, and after about fifteen minutes, I burst forth that the government's practice of violence inculcates it in a society, that it is demonstrable that the death penalty has no deterrent value, that we're the only industrialized democracy that still uses it, that all Europe sees us as barbaric, and that we find ourselves among an increasingly exclusive and repulsive group of countries that still uses it—us and Iran, Iraq, Saudi Arabia, and China.

Red roared with laughter. "I knew it," he said. "I knew it. You've just been toying with her. I knew if I pushed your buttons you would deliver a pontification. That's your name: Ralph Pontification Temple."

I had to laugh. He's got my number. We've got each other's number.

I have trouble with Red's views on a number of issues, and certainly with some history. But we see eye to eye on a lot. I've followed his career, and the truth is, Red is one of the finest cops in the country.

On June 2, 2001, I made the pilgrimage down to Miami for his retirement event. Just before I went down, he asked if I'd like to join all the police and city brass that would be singing his praise.

Before an audience of 400 police officials and rank-and-file, plus the mayor, city officials, some judges, and Red's children, their spouses, and his grandchildren, I told the story of "The ACLU Lawyer and the Cop":

* * *

In the summer of 1958, two young men, twenty-five years old, came together in their home town, Miami Beach, after having been apart for seven years.

Even at that time, over four decades earlier, these two were old friends.

They had been buddies since the third grade. They had: been patrol boys and Boy Scouts together; done World War II newspaper collection drives together; worked together on their first jobs delivering newspapers; studied for their Bar Mitzvahs together at the Beth Jacob Synagogue at 3rd and Washington Avenue on Miami Beach. They graduated together from South Beach Elementary School, from Ida M. Fisher Junior High, and, in 1951, from Miami Beach Senior High.

After high school, they went their separate ways. But they came together again when they both got out of the armed forces, one from the Air Force and the other from the Army. It was summer; they were about to begin their careers in September of that year, one embarking on a career in law, and the other preparing to hit the streets, for the Metropolitan Public Safety Department of Dade County, as a rookie cop.

And that last season of their youths, the summer of 1958, was the final bonding that would keep them close for a lifetime . . . despite their seemingly conflicting careers.

For the one who became a cop rose steadily through the ranks, to sergeant, to lieutenant, to captain, right on up to assistant director.

And the other became a lawyer for the American Civil Liberties Union of Washington, D.C., and spent much of his time criticizing and suing the police.

Through the years, these two have found a million ways to jerk each other's chain, arguing incessantly, sometimes quietly, sometimes ferociously, about every issue of law enforcement and civil liberties you can imagine.

But, in the end, blood is thicker than water, and friendship can transcend politics . . . and police work and civil liberties best serve the community when they go hand in hand.

Today, the former ACLU lawyer stands before you to salute his dear friend.

Red, you are a fundamentally decent and devoted man who exemplifies the best in police work and the best in public service. You've had the talent, the drive, and the heart that it takes to be a great cop, and the judgment to make the right calls and to influence and inspire all those under your command. You've been a credit and a blessing to the department and to the community.

And so, old friend, we salute you.

PART II

CIVIL RIGHTS WARRIOR

WITH SALLY BROWN IN CAMELOT
1960

John F. Kennedy's election brought a breath of fresh air to Washington, D.C., in 1960. Sally and I were married in July of that year, and somehow the romance got caught up in the campaign. Sally knew Kennedy from Capitol Hill, having been an aide to another Senate Democrat, Vance Hartke of Indiana. When Senator Kennedy won the nomination, Sally went to work for the campaign on a public relations team. During the first TV screening of one of Kennedy's speeches, he spotted her across the room, and called out, "Hey, Sally Brown." She walked over to greet him.

"You're going to beat Nixon, aren't you—you've just got to," Sally whispered.

"I've got to. He shouldn't be president. He's a bad man," Kennedy whispered back.

The night before Kennedy's inauguration in January 1961, a huge snow storm hit Washington, snarling traffic and making it impossible for us to drive home. Sally and I, stuck downtown, ended up sleeping on a couch in the office of Monroe Freedman, a friend of mine on the faculty of George Washington University Law School, where I taught and Sally was a student. Having escaped detection of illicit fraternization during our six-month courtship, it was odd to have a custodian walk in on us in Monroe's office that night, and a relief to be able to assure him that the student was my wife.

We stood in the vast crowd huddled together in the twenty-degree weather at the U.S. Capitol, and watched while the bare-headed, white-haired Robert Frost read a poem. Then the president spoke of the torch passing to a new generation, and how we would not shirk our duty to defend freedom anywhere in the world.

We believed it in those days, and the new president did not have to wait long before his mettle was tested by the Soviets in the Cuban missile confrontation.

Washington enjoyed the influx of waves of intellectuals and liberals and people who thought it was possible to build a great nation and a humane world. Our hearts were truly young and gay, and our lives full of hope and joy. Our faith was not entirely betrayed. It was a good marriage that was to last twenty-one years, and find us, another twenty years after our divorce and well into our second marriages, on the telephone together on July 17 wishing each other a happy forty-first anniversary.

ST. AUGUSTINE 1964
1964

Originally published in Flavour: Black Florida Life & Style, *Spring 2005*

"You nigger-lovin' Jew lawyers, we know what yer doin'. We waitin' f'yew, yew gonna get it. Hear me, boy?"

"Yeah, sure," I replied into the telephone. "You get that, Mr. Cummings—you get the FBI trace on that?"

The bluff worked; the anonymous caller hung up abruptly. There was no Cummings, no FBI.

Contrary to the 1988 film *Mississippi Burning*, in which Gene Hackman is the FBI agent who puts the muscle on the Ku Klux Klan and rescues the helpless black community, the FBI's role in the civil rights battles was unreliable at best and subversive at worst. Almost one-third of the FBI agents in the South were themselves Southerners, steeped in the culture of segregation, and most of the rest were detached, passively resisting the struggle of African-Americans. The FBI's observe-and-report mode is exemplified by the FBI's Ku Klux Klan operative who sat by while three other Klansmen with him, in a drive-by shooting, killed Viola Liuzzo, a forty-two-year-old white housewife from Detroit who was a volunteer in an Alabama voter registration drive. FBI director J. Edgar Hoover conducted surveillance of Dr. Martin Luther King Jr.'s adulterous af-

fairs, hoping to destroy his leadership. The FBI didn't res-
cue Southern blacks; black people themselves waged the
war with hundreds of Northern whites like Mrs. Liuzzo
coming to lend a hand.

Going South

That was why I was in St. Augustine, Florida, for two
weeks in August 1964. I was thirty-two years old, eight
years out of law school. After graduating in 1956, I worked
at the NAACP Legal Defense Fund in New York City for
Thurgood Marshall, the leading civil rights lawyer of the
time and later the first black Supreme Court justice. I was
drafted and spent two years in the Army at Ft. Bragg, North
Carolina, followed by four years of teaching law. In 1962, I
went to work for Arnold, Fortas & Porter, one of Washington's largest law firms.

In July 1964, Richard Sobol, another young associate
in the firm, introduced me to Henry Schwarzschild, who
had recruited Sobol for a stint of volunteer lawyering with
the civil rights movement in New Orleans. Henry, with his
sophisticated European manner and accent, though not a
lawyer, was a passionate advocate, working out of New
York City for the Lawyers Constitutional Defense Committee. The LCDC had recently been formed to cope with
what was to be the hottest summer of the civil rights wars.

Thomas Hilbink's 112-page history of the LCDC cred-
its its formation mainly to Mel Wulf, legal director of the
American Civil Liberties Union, and Carl Rachlin, general
counsel of the Congress of Racial Equality. The mass arrests of black protesters were overwhelming the few black
lawyers in the South who would dare take on such cases.
The few white lawyers who did so, like Bill Higgs in Mississippi and Chuck Morgan in Birmingham, were run out of
town. Hilbink's history also describes the political prob-

lems in the formation of LCDC. The National Lawyers' Guild, although active in civil rights in the South, was excluded because some thought the group was tainted with Communism. Jack Greenberg of the NAACP Legal Defense Fund (Inc. Fund) was resistant to the formation of LCDC for what Hilbink describes as reasons of "turf," and also because the Inc. Fund's approach was to develop test cases methodically and carefully, not to send in platoons of volunteers inexperienced in civil rights litigation.

Hilbink tells us that in the spring of 1964, Wulf and Rachlin assembled a half dozen organizations, including the National Council of Churches, the American Jewish Congress, the American Jewish Committee, and the NAACP Inc. Fund. Each contributed money or other resources, Henry Schwarzschild was hired to round up and coordinate the operations, and in May 1964 the LCDC began seeking volunteers. The new organization oriented its recruits with a critical guiding principle: lawyers were going South, not to direct the civil rights movement, but to assist local African-Americans in the directions and activities they chose for themselves. This principle—that the lawyer works for the client to achieve the client's ends, rather than dictating to the client—was a luxury that had all too often been reserved for the corporate world that could pay its lawyers and therefore direct their actions. Now the civil rights movement, too, would have that autonomy. On June 6–7, 1964, over one hundred volunteer lawyers attended a training and orientation session at Columbia Law School, and shortly after that, the first contingents were on their way South.

The idea was to fill the ranks by asking Northern lawyers to spend their vacations on two-week lawyering gigs in the hot spots: Birmingham, Jackson, Memphis, New Orleans, and St. Augustine. The multiple civil rights defenses and lawsuits were conducted relay-race style, with each team of volunteers passing the litigation baton every week or two to a new team just arriving. Naturally, the twists, turns, and dynamics of even routine legal actions are too complicated to work with a constant changing of the lawyers, let alone the often complex civil rights cases conducted in hostile territory. So it would never work—any experienced litigator knew that. But it did work. Powerfully.

On April 12, 1963, the eight leading white clergymen of Birmingham, Alabama—six ministers, a rabbi, and a bishop— issued a public statement urging Martin Luther King to call off civil rights demonstrations in that city. The national media had been televising police and thugs viciously attacking peaceful black protesters. The clergymen emphasized reform efforts that were underway. "In Birmingham," they said, "recent public events have given indication that we all have an opportunity for a new constructive and realistic approach to racial problems." They said that Dr. King and other "outside agitators" were succeeding only in provoking violent responses and interfering with their reform efforts. From prison, Dr. King responded in his classic "Letter From Birmingham Jail," a declaration of what the civil rights movement was about. Passages of that eloquent manifesto keep recurring in my memories of that summer. In response to the charge that he was an outside agitator, Dr. King wrote:

> *I am here, along with several members of my staff, because we were invited here . . . Beyond this, I am in Birmingham because injustice is here. Just as the eighth century prophets left their little villages and carried their "thus saith the Lord" far beyond the boundaries of their home town, and just as the Apostle Paul left his little village of Tarsus and carried the gospel of Jesus*

Christ to practically every hamlet and city of the Graeco-Roman world, I too am compelled to carry the gospel of freedom beyond my particular home town.

Those whites who went South in the 1960s were fired up, driven by the injustices of segregation, suppression, and violence, and inspired by Dr. King.

I cannot sit idly by in Atlanta and not be concerned about what happens in Birmingham. Injustice anywhere is a threat to justice everywhere . . . Whatever affects one directly, affects all indirectly. Never again can we afford to live with the narrow, provincial "outside agitator" idea. Anyone who lives inside the United States can never be considered an outsider anywhere in this country.

On the Sunday morning of August 2, 1964, on the flight from my home in Washington, D.C., down to Florida, I was exhilarated and nervous. There had been no shootings or bombings in St. Augustine for several months. I did not really expect danger, but my wife Sally, carrying our first child due in seven weeks, was worried when she saw me off at the airport, and on the flight down I found that I was too. The summer before, Klansmen set off a bomb in a black Birmingham church that killed four children, aged twelve to sixteen. Only six weeks earlier, on June 21, 1964, a sheriff in Philadelphia, Mississippi led a lynch mob that kidnapped and murdered three young civil rights workers—black Mississippian James Chaney and two white Northerners, Michael Schwerner and Andrew Goodman. In St. Augustine, protesters marching out of the black section to the historic slave market in the center of the city had been attacked by a white mob swinging chains and clubs. Newspapers across the country had carried a front-page photograph showing the owner of a St. Augustine motel pouring acid into the swimming pool where black teenagers were conducting a "swim-in."

What Dr. King had to say from the Birmingham jail was not far off the mark for all the major Southern cities:

> Birmingham is probably the most thoroughly segregated city in the United States. Its ugly record of police brutality is known in every section of this country. Its unjust treatment of Negroes in the courts is a notorious reality. There have been more unsolved bombings of Negro homes and churches in Birmingham than any city in this nation.

St. Augustine is close to the east coast of Florida, up near the top of that long state, and calls itself "The Ancient City," ostensibly the nation's oldest. At eleven-thirty a.m. the plane landed in Jacksonville, forty miles south of the Georgia border and, after Miami, the second largest city in Florida. Eric Chamblis, a volunteer law student from California, met and drove me the thirty miles south to St. Augustine. On the way, Eric described the office operation, the housing, and the activities in progress. At the office I met my two teammates, Alvin Dorfman, about thirty, from Long Island, New York, who had been there for a week, and Martin Fox, about forty, who had arrived from New Jersey the night before.

Al Dorfman briefed us on the ongoing actions in the local courts and in the federal court in Jacksonville, and guided us through the files of the most imminent. We divided assignments for the next few days. Marty Fox and I were then introduced to Dr. Robert Hayling, whose dental office was our base of operations—where several days later I received the threatening telephone call described above.

Dr. Hayling was the leader of the local SCLC, Dr. King's Southern Christian Leadership Conference. The dental office was located in a one-story building just big enough for an anteroom, two rooms with dental chairs, and one with a desk. The anteroom was spacious and had been converted to the lawyering business by the addition of two desks, a couple of small work tables, three four-drawer filing cabinets, and extra phone lines. Dr. Hayling's patients did not seem to mind, making their way around the bustling lawyers and law students. The office was situated just across the railroad tracks that were the borderline between St. Augustine proper and Lincolnsville, which is what the "colored" section of the city was called.

Southern towns and cities always had colored sections. African-Americans were allowed to come into the regular city only to work for whites. Public places in the white section always had two sets of restrooms and drinking fountains, marked *white* and *colored*, and black people were confined to a small area at the back of buses. Except for the black ghettoes, African-Americans could not dine at restaurants, go to the movies, or even snack at drugstore lunch counters.

Growing up in Miami, I was revolted by that culture. In an episode when I was twelve, a group of us were standing near the rear of a crowded bus on our way to a Saturday matinee at the Dixie Theater, when a white man, having trouble squeezing past a black man, suddenly shouted, "Out of my way, you goddamn nigger, don't you know to get out of the way for a white man, goddamn you!" and, turning to us, "You boys ought to help me whip this goddamn nigger to teach him a lesson!" The black man appeared embarrassed and frightened. No one said anything, the white man got off the bus, and we went on to our movie. When I was finally home alone at the end of the day, I cried out the humiliation and rage I'd bottled up all day over the incident.

Dr. Robert Hayling

Dr. Hayling was a big man, about six feet three inches tall with broad shoulders, short-cropped hair, a wide face and thin mustache. His eyes and voice were soft, mellifluous, and reassuring. He was also something of a risk-taker. Less than a year earlier, on September 18, 1963, he and three friends had spied on a Ku Klux Klan rally in an open field at the edge of some woods just outside St. Augustine. Crouching in the woods, they had watched as the crowd of several hundred, many in Klan hoods and robes, lit a large cross then listened to a lengthy harangue by one of the infamous Klan figures of the times, Connie Lynch, a self-styled minister from Alabama. Reverend Irvin Cheney, a white minister who was assistant director of the Florida Human Relations Council, monitored the event from the middle of the crowd where he appeared to be just another Klan supporter. Cheney wrote a detailed description of the event, including Connie Lynch's speech. Excerpts of that diatribe provide a glimpse of the pathology of hatred:

> My friends, I want to share with you something of the history, the glorious history of the Klan. The Klan was born out of bloodshed, out of a real need to protect the Southern white man from the carpetbaggers—the Jew carpetbaggers. You know, of course, that the carpetbaggers was Jews, and they come down here and teamed up with the niggers and tried to take everything the white man had. But they learned that the white man would not take this lying down.

Lynch called upon white people to take up arms to defend their way of life. Then, Reverend Cheney reported,

Lynch addressed the church bombing that killed the four black girls in Birmingham:

If they can find these fellows who done that, they ought to pin medals on them. Someone said, "Ain't it a shame that them little children was killed?" Well, in the first place, they ain't little. They're fourteen or fifteen years old—old enough to have venereal diseases, and I'll be surprised if all of 'em didn't have one or more. In the second place, they weren't children. Children are little people, little human beings, and that means white people. There's little monkeys, but you don't call them children. They're just little monkeys. There's little dogs and cats and apes and baboons and skunks and there's also little niggers. But they ain't children. They're just little niggers.

Lynch stirred the crowd and himself:

And in the third place, it wasn't no shame they was killed. Why? Because when I go out to kill rattlesnakes, I don't make no difference between little rattlesnakes and big rattlesnakes, because I know it is the nature of all rattlesnakes to be my enemies and to poison me if they can. So I kill 'em all, and if there's four less niggers tonight, then I say, "Good for whoever planted the bomb." We're all better off.

As a "minister," Lynch also addressed the theological issues:

Some people say that we'll all be in heaven together. The hell we will! Only God's family will be in heaven, and niggers and Jews ain't God's family. Ain't gonna be no animals in heaven, and ain't gonna be no sons of perdition there. It's just a shame some people brought these black animals over here, animals highly enough developed so that their seed can mix with your seed . . .

Some of the niggers say, "We want to go to your churches." There ain't but one manly, Christian thing to do when they try, and that is to meet 'em at the church house door with a base- ball bat and beat their brains out.

Reverend Cheney reported that Lynch then turned his attention to Dr. Hayling himself, who was secretly wit- nessing the event:

I'll tell you something else. You've got a nigger in St. Augustine that ought not to live—that burr-headed bastard of a dentist. He's got no right to live at all, let alone walk up and down your streets and breathe the white man's free air. He ought to wake up tomorrow morning with a bullet between his eyes. If you were half the men you claim to be, you'd kill him before sunup.

Reverend Cheney related how Lynch went on for an hour and fifteen minutes. The next speaker was dull, and the crowd, growing bored, dwindled down to about a hundred. At that moment, when something was needed to enliven those remaining, they got it. Dr. Hayling and his three companions were caught at gunpoint by Klansmen coming up behind them in the woods.

The four were hauled before the crowd, which howled for their blood. Several women screamed, "Cut off their balls!" As Dr. Hayling and his three companions were being beaten bloody with chains, baseball bats, and ax handles, Reverend Cheney heard one robed Klanswoman whisper to her husband, "Go get the headchopper and the rope, and for God's sake, take off your robe and leave it in the car. You don't want to mess it up." Cheney eased his way out of the crowd to go for help.

He got the police, who came and pulled the beaten victims out of there. All four were hospitalized, some for as long as twelve days. The mob had broken Dr. Hayling's wrists. Typical of Southern "law enforcement," the police made minor charges against only four of the Klansmen, who were then exonerated by a racist magistrate, G. Marvin Grier. Dr. Hayling and his three companions were charged with assault, trespass, and other crimes. Among the piles of civil rights leaflets around Dr. Hayling's office was one with a photograph of him propped up in a hospital bed, his wrists in casts. I was glad to learn from his firm grip when we met that his hands were all right.

Dr. Hayling described to Marty and me the office routines, the town, the daily marches and protest activity, and our housing. Each of us was assigned to stay with residents of Lincolnsville who had offered to put up the Northern visitors. We would walk down the poorly paved streets without sidewalks to the old wooden shacks of our hosts, as much as a mile from our dental office headquarters. My room was in the house of a small dark-skinned old lady who lived there with her lovely nineteen-year-old granddaughter, a domestic worker. They were delighted to have me, and their affection, the old bed, and the bathtub were great comforts during my stay.

Dr. Hayling concluded his introductory talk to us with safety cautions. "Don't ever go into St. Ow-gostine," he drawled, referring to the white section of the city, "except in the daytime, and then only in the company of someone else. Always let someone here know where you're going and when you'll be back. Here you're safe; you can go anywhere in Lincolnsville any time of the day or night. Everyone in town knows why you boys are here." He added, "Use to be that the Manucys would come riding through here at night, firing guns, setting fires, raising hell."

Halstead "Hoss" Manucy, a horse-faced man strutting around in a cowboy hat and boots, his huge belly overhanging his belt line, led a family of brothers and cousins who were the core of the local Ku Klux Klan, masquerading under the name "The Ancient City Gun & Hunting Club."

Dr. Hayling said, "They shotgunned my house last summer, and wounded some boys standing outside. And they've burned up a few homes with Molotov cocktails. Just six months ago, they came through here and shot up my house again. Killed my dog, and almost hit my pregnant wife." Then his face turned gentler and his voice softer and he continued, "But all that stopped three months ago. They came in across the railroad tracks one night in a pickup truck. Chuck Manucy was driving, and Tom Morris [a pseudonym] was sitting next to him with a loaded shotgun across his lap, when a bullet hit him right here." Dr. Hayling pressed his index finger firmly and flatly between his eyes at the middle of the forehead. "They claim Johnny-Lee Brown [a pseudonym] did it, and they been holding him in jail on a murder charge. But they've got no proof; he'll get out." A slight smile. "So they don't come through Lincolnsville anymore; you're safe here."

For the first few days, every time I stepped out the door of Dr. Hayling's office, within, say, a shotgun blast of white St. Augustine, a frozen sensation would ripple down my chest and stomach. Throughout my stay I was on edge each time I had to venture into the white section of the city. But I could walk home alone sometimes as late as two in the morning, feeling completely safe. Violence, of course, was not the way of the civil rights movement. Martin Luther King drew his strength from his Christian faith and from the inspiration of Mahatma Gandhi and, like Gandhi, preached nonviolence. But I was grateful to the maverick whose gunshot into a Manucy car had made me feel safe in Lincolnsville.

Judge Bryan Simpson

Marty Fox, Al Dorfman, and I got going the next day, Monday, preparing legal documents and visiting the local courthouse in St. Augustine and the federal court in Jacksonville, about an hour's drive away. The office staff of the clerk of the local court bristled; we were definitely in hostile territory. With care, we pushed for the files we'd come to inspect, and got them.

The federal court in Jacksonville, formally called the United States District Court for the Middle District of Florida, was different. The judge of that court, Bryan Simpson, white-haired and maybe fifty-five, was a born-and-bred Southern gentleman. He had responded early on to civil rights lawyers with disparaging comments and unfavorable rulings. But the mounting injustices and violence against black people that were repeatedly brought to Judge Simpson's attention had a profound effect on him, and he had changed.

Judge Simpson warmly welcomed us into his oak-paneled office, shook our hands, and waved us into chairs in front of his large desk. "So you're the new team," he said with a smile. "Where are you gentlemen from?"

We chatted in this comfortable fashion for some time before coming to the main order of business. We were there to enforce the desegregation of public facilities required by the newly enacted Civil Rights Act of 1964. This new federal statute had been passed by Congress and signed into law by President Lyndon Johnson on July 2, just a month earlier, a major victory for the civil rights movement. The new battle was to force compliance with the law, to dismantle the 300-year-old Jim Crow tradition. In St. Augustine and other key cities in the South, black people were pressing forward, going to restaurants, hotels, and other places of public accommodation, no longer having to sit-in, because for the first time in the one hundred years since the Civil War, the law was on their side.

At first, St. Augustine businesses began to comply with the new law and provide nondiscriminatory service. They reversed course when they found themselves the object of demonstrations and threats by the Ku Klux Klan. Earlier in the summer, our LCDC predecessors had filed suit against seventeen St. Augustine restaurants and motels, asking the federal court to order them to obey the law, and seeking an injunction against Hoss Manucy and his gang to restrain them from intimidating the business owners and the black people seeking service. Judge Simpson had conducted a hearing the week before Marty and I arrived. We asked what the judge was going to do. He said, "I have read all the documents and, at last week's hearing, listened to the arguments of both sides. I'm ready to rule, and on Wednesday I'm going to issue the order you fellows have been after."

"Do you want us here for that?" asked Marty Fox. "Are we and the opposing lawyers going to have to be prepared with anything?"

"Not right away," answered Judge Simpson. "I'll wait a day or two after I've issued the order to give the businesses a chance to ask me to stay the order so that they have time to file an appeal from my ruling."

"We don't think they should be able to delay compliance with the order, Your Honor," Marty said. "It's plainly right, and they have had plenty of time to get ready for this."

"Just the same," the judge replied, "I'm leaning toward letting them have a stay so they can appeal. There's a similar case going from the U.S. District Court in Atlanta up to the United States Supreme Court. I will want to see what the Supreme Court is going to do with that. In the meantime, I think you all should wait and not have your people pushing it." In short, Judge Simpson wanted no more demonstrations or African-Americans asking for service at white places while the resolution of this case was pending. He wanted things to remain as calm as possible in St. Augustine. Marty and I had anticipated this and had discussed it with Dr. Hayling.

"They're pretty impatient at this point, Your Honor," I said. "I don't know that they'll be willing to wait any longer now that the law is clear."

"Sure," said Judge Simpson, "I understand that. But they may still have to wait a little longer, just to let this lawsuit run its course. Anyway, after I've issued the injunction, I'll hear arguments from both sides about a stay."

Marty and I were exchanging glances, trying to keep ourselves aligned during the dialogue. At this point we felt it was time to stop pushing. We stayed awhile longer, continuing to get to know Judge Simpson. We left quite happy; we had good news for Dr. Hayling: the injunctions against the motels, the restaurants, and the Klan were coming the day after tomorrow.

Our next stop was at the office of one of our bosses, Earl Johnson, an African-American, the leading civil rights attorney in Jacksonville. He asked that one of the three of us stay in Jacksonville to work with him on a daily basis. We clustered amongst ourselves and found that none of us wanted to leave St. Augustine. Al Dorfman finally said he'd do it.

Marty Fox and I spent Tuesday morning fumbling with the files, which, with all the lawyers streaming in and out of town, were a mess. We had lunch at a diner across the street from Dr. Hayling's office, a place that became our social center whenever there was time to spare in the days that followed. There we got to hobnob with the folks of Lincolnsville, and to eat the biggest, richest peach ice-cream cones I've ever had.

In the afternoon, Marty and I went to the local county courthouse in St. Augustine to check court records on some pending lawsuits. We again met resistance from a woman in the clerk's office, but she remained pleasant even while digging in her heels, and finally yielded to Marty's gentle pressure without getting riled.

We also wanted to get a look at Judge Charles C. Mathis Jr., the county judge who we had been warned was hard-core Southern resistance. In July 1963, after seven African-American children under fourteen years of age had been arrested for picketing against a whites-only restaurant, Judge Mathis required their parents to sign promises that the children would not participate in any more protests. When the parents of four refused to sign, Judge Mathis had the children locked up in the county jail.

We slipped into his courtroom while he was conducting the trial of a white man charged with possessing moonshine whiskey—liquor distilled and sold without benefit of tax stamps, in violation of state and federal laws. The defense lawyer, being creative in a normally routine case, cross-examined the arresting police officer, asking him how he knew the moonshine in issue was illegal. "I never heard of legal moonshine," answered the officer. The lawyer then produced a jar of clear liquid labeled *Georgia Moonshine* that bore the required tax stamps, and asked the officer to smell the contents. The policeman sniffed the jar, shook his head, grinned sheepishly, and acknowledged, "Yep, that's moonshine all right," thereby undermining his testimony that moonshine is always illegal and allowing the lawyer the classic gesture of turning away with a triumphant, "No more questions." Marty and I did not wait around to be disappointed, convinced from his comments that Judge Mathis was going to find the accused guilty anyway.

That night we traveled in a convoy of three cars from Lincolnsville to church meetings in the nearby cities of Gainesville and Ocala. Southern black churches, normally lively, were tame compared to the energy we saw that night. Standing, swaying, sweating, shouting, Amening, arms locked, singing "We Shall Overcome" and "We Shall Not Be Moved" and "Let My People Go," the people were ablaze with the jubilation of the Call—the Call with which the preachers, echoing Dr. King, roused their followers: "Free at last, free at last, great G-d Almighty, I'm free at last!" They were, as Eli Wiesel once called nineteenth-century Hassids, souls on fire.

We stayed late, as the communities prepared for Dr. King's return to St. Augustine the next day. Two months earlier, on June 11, 1964, Dr. King had been arrested here for sitting in at a restaurant. He had left jail two days later to accept an honorary degree at Yale, and prior to his departure had promised St. Augustine "a long hot summer" of demonstrations and legal actions. Now he was returning, on August 5, to hold a press conference coinciding with Judge Simpson's order requiring the town's hotels and restaurants to comply with the new law.

The court order was significant beyond its immediate purpose of opening hotels and restaurants to African-Americans. It was aimed at the power structure that had held the walls of segregation in place throughout the South: the respectable citizens of the business communities and their shock troops—the racist police and the Klan. The aim of the civil rights movement was to force the white establishment to exert its power to open the doors of public

places to African-Americans and to put a stop to the violence—in effect, to call off their dogs. That was what Dr.
King was addressing in his Birmingham jail letter. In answer to the call of the eight white clergymen to wait, Dr.
King had written:

> *For years now I have heard the word "Wait!" It rings in the ear
> of every Negro with a piercing familiarity . . . We have waited
> more than three hundred and forty years for our constitutional
> and God-given rights . . .*

And described what racism feels like on the receiving
end—

> *I guess it is easy for those who have never felt the stinging darts
> of segregation to say wait. But when you have seen vicious mobs
> lynch your mothers and fathers at will and drown your sisters
> and brothers at whim; when you have seen hate-filled police-
> men curse, kick, brutalize and even kill your black brothers
> and sisters with impunity . . .*

The economic suffocation—

> *. . . when you see the vast majority of your twenty million black
> brothers smothering in an air-tight cage of poverty in the midst
> of an affluent society . . .*

The crippling effect on children—

> *. . . when you suddenly find your tongue twisted and your
> speech stammering as you seek to explain to your six-year-old
> daughter why she can't go to the public amusement park that
> has just been advertised on television, and see tears welling up
> in her little eyes when she is told that Funtown is closed to col-*

ored children, and see the depressing clouds of inferiority begin to form in her little mental sky, and see her begin to distort her little personality by unconsciously developing a bitterness toward white people; when you have to concoct an answer for a five-year-old son asking in agonizing pathos: "Daddy, why do white people treat colored people so mean?" . . .

The burdens on movement—

. . . when you take a cross-country drive and find it necessary to sleep night after night in the uncomfortable corners of your automobile because no motel will accept you . . .

And, finally and most oppressive, the dehumanization—

. . . when you are humiliated day in and day out by nagging signs reading "white" men and "colored"; when your first name becomes "nigger" and your middle name becomes "boy" (however old you are) and your last name becomes "John," and when your wife and mother are never given the respected title "Mrs."; when you are harried by day and haunted by night by the fact that you are a Negro, living constantly at tiptoe stance never quite knowing what to expect next, and plagued with inner fears and outer resentments; when you are forever fighting a degenerating sense of "nobodiness"—then you will understand why we find it difficult to wait.

Following the church rallies, we arrived back in Lincolnsville about six-thirty a.m. Wednesday morning, got a few hours sleep, and were back in Dr. Hayling's office at eleven. I got together with Henry Schwarzschild, who had recruited me for this stint and who had come down from New York for the press conference. In the early afternoon when we arrived at the church, Henry said, "Would you like to meet Dr. King?" Walking around the side of the church, we approached a group of men.

Henry introduced me to Dr. King and to his chief assistant, Hosea Williams. We shook hands. Dr. King was shorter and slightly stockier than I expected. The four of us walked into a small room of the church, where Dr. King invited me to sit with him while the others got busy preparing for the press conference. We chatted for a few minutes before he was called away. I cannot recall a word that was said; I remember only his big open face, his gentle wide eyes.

At one p.m. Dr. King, then Henry, spoke to the media, there in full force, and hailed Judge Simpson's order against the businesses and the Manucy gang.

As the press conference was winding down, Eric Chamblis, the law student who met me at the airport three days earlier, introduced me to Reverend Johnson, an African-American minister from Daytona Beach, forty miles south of St. Augustine. He told us that three nights earlier four black teenagers seeking service at a "white" drive-in restaurant had been chased and assaulted by several white men, who then called the police and had them arrest the four youngsters plus five others nearby. All nine were charged with disorderly conduct, and seven were still in jail. They were scheduled to be charged in city court the next morning.

Eric and I hit the typewriters in Dr. Hayling's office and prepared a two-page "Petition for Removal." This legal device was one of the magic bullets in the arsenal of materials which the LCDC furnished to its volunteers before we came South. The petition invoked a previously little-known federal law which allowed those who claimed that local courts would not protect their civil rights to "remove" their cases to the federal courts. Once it was filed, the local court had no power to act until the federal court decided whether the removal petition was well founded. The force of the petition was that, just by filing it in federal court, we could temporarily halt the Daytona proceedings until the dust had settled. It was a power play to let the locals know that they could be called to account. Eric and I drove to Jacksonville and got the petition filed by five-fifteen p.m. The next day we would serve notice on the Daytona Beach prosecutor and judge that the cases against the nine black teens had been removed to federal court.

That night we all attended a rally at the church in Lincolnsville. Reverend King and Hosea Williams spoke with stirring passion. Then Henry Schwarzschild, breathing fire, railed against the grand jury for dragging its feet in investigating and proposing solutions for the civil rights crisis in St. Augustine. Grand juries usually consider only specific criminal charges, but in some states they are authorized to address problems more broadly. Dr. King and Dr. Hayling had targeted the grand jury as a mechanism to pressure St. Augustine's political and business establishments. In April, Dr. Hayling had even filed a lengthy petition detailing the oppression of St. Augustine's black community with the Organization of American States. St. Augustine was placed in the international as well as the national spotlight.

The Tide Turns

At seven a.m. the next morning, Thursday, August 6, Eric and I left for Daytona Beach, arriving at eight-thirty for a meeting with Reverend Johnson and a local black attorney, Joseph Hatchett. We then went to the courthouse where we met with the Daytona Beach city attorney, Louis Ossinsky Jr., a young Jewish man who displayed none of the usual hostility to us outside agitators. I told him we were appearing for the nine boys scheduled for arraignment that morning and served him with a copy of the federal removal petition we had just filed. He said he would not oppose the suspension of the city court proceedings or the release the nine accused.

Ossinsky then accompanied me to the chambers of Judge Robert Durden, the Municipal Court judge, explained why I was there, informed the judge of the petition removing the cases to federal court, and said that the city had no objection. Ossinsky thus created an ambiance in which I could, without offending the judge, serve him with the document which deprived him of authority in the case by alleging that he would not provide a fair trial. It was agreed that the teenagers would be released on low bonds.

At 9:45 a.m., Judge Durden convened the court, our case was called, and the nine youths were brought before the bench, seven in prison clothes. Hatchett and I stepped forward. I was fulfilling a fantasy I'd had since, at seventeen, I'd read Haywood Patterson's *Scottsboro Boy*, the story of nine black youths framed for rape and sentenced to death in Scottsboro, Alabama in 1932. Judge Durden permitted me to appear as counsel, and to announce the removal petition for the record. Ossinsky said that the city agreed with us that this court had no jurisdiction to proceed, and the judge said that no further steps would be taken pending the federal court's action. Then, on my request, the judge reduced the bonds to $100 each.

When the court session ended, I addressed the parents and relatives of the teenagers, and later, after they were released about eleven-thirty a.m., the youths themselves, on our intention to follow through with this matter as a civil rights case. They were awed and grateful. I was too.

In the afternoon, we met with Louis Ossinsky and the city manager, Norman Hickey. I suggested that the St. Augustine furor began with incidents like this one. They said they would get together with the mayor and the City Commission and recommend issuing special orders to the police, who they acknowledged were a problem. They agreed to consider dropping the charges against the nine youngsters, and I said if they did so, we would refrain from suing over the arrests. Ossinsky and Hickey emphasized that they did not want Daytona Beach to turn into another St. Augustine.

That evening back in the office, we prepared a written statement for the African-American members of a biracial committee appointed by the grand jury to address St. Augustine's racial problems.

On Friday afternoon, August 7, we went to Jacksonville and appeared before Judge Simpson in his chambers. As anticipated, the lawyers for the restaurants and hotels asked the judge to stay his August 5 order to serve black people until their appeal to the United States Court of Appeals for the Fifth Circuit was decided. That could take weeks or months. After listening to us—Earl Johnson, Marty Fox, and I all spoke—Judge Simpson denied the stay. But he said that, depending on what the Supreme Court did in a similar case in Atlanta, he might give the defendants a *limited* stay for just twelve days to let them ask the appeals court for a stay. Judge Simpson then telephoned the clerk's office of the United States Supreme Court in Washington and asked when Justice Black was expected to rule on a request for a stay in the Atlanta case. He was informed that Justice Black's ruling was expected on Monday. Judge Simpson, brushing aside my suggestion that further delay might revive Klan resistance, leaned on us, and we reluctantly agreed to hold off further demonstrations over the weekend until noon on Monday.

Early the next morning, Saturday, Marty Fox returned

to New Jersey, and Al Dorfman took the weekend off in Tampa. I went to Jacksonville and spent an hour and a half chatting with Judge Simpson about all the civil rights matters in the works, both in and out of the courts. I showed him a newspaper report that the restaurants' and hotels' effort to get a stay was intended to buy enough time to convert their businesses into "private" clubs, so they could continue to exclude blacks. I told the judge there was no way we could delay testing beyond Monday, that we had caught hell for agreeing to hold off until then. The judge grinned, and I sensed that he would not push us further to hold off on testing and protests. The judge said he thought the private club maneuver would be broken by test cases. We talked about Hoss Manucy and whether he was complying with Judge Simpson's August 5 order directing him to call off his hoods. The judge said he did not have much confidence in a biracial committee whose black members had been selected by the white establishment.

That evening, Fred Martin, a white worker for the Southern Christian Leadership Conference, drove me to the airport in Jacksonville to meet Alvin Bronstein, a lawyer with a one-man practice in upstate New York who was replacing Marty Fox. I didn't know it then, but that was the beginning of a lifelong friendship. The day ended with Dr. Hayling taking me to hang out at a Lincolnsville café with some of the locals, ordinary people who'd gotten caught up in the movement.

On Sunday, Al Bronstein, pulling me along with him, jumped headlong into the chaos that we called files. Working all day under his guidance, we at last got the office into intelligible shape.

On Monday, August 10, Al and I spent the afternoon in Judge Simpson's chambers waiting for Justice Black's ruling in the Atlanta civil rights cases. Finally, just before five p.m., the Supreme Court clerk telephoned Judge Simpson and read Justice Black's ruling denying a stay of a U.S. District Court order, forcing Atlanta restaurants and hotels to obey the Civil Rights Act of 1964 and open their doors to African-Americans. At last, Judge Simpson denied a stay. St. Augustine businesses had to serve blacks or face contempt-of-court penalties.

That same afternoon, black citizens resumed their testing of white facilities in St. Augustine. The law-enforcement authorities, as usual, were of no help in protecting African-Americans seeking service. The FBI, as usual, said they were there only as observers, and it was up to the local authorities to maintain order. The state troopers said they too were only observers and it was up to the city police to maintain order. The city police said they would not enforce the Civil Rights Act because it was a federal law.

That's why it sometimes took brigades of federal troops or Northern lawyers to enforce the law in the South.

As matters turned out, there was only one incident that day. A group of white men taunted two black teenagers who had just been served at a Dairy Queen, and one of the men, a Manucy named Herbert, threw an ice-cream cone onto the shoulder of a youth named Willie Singleton. That the Klan had been reduced to verbal taunts and ice-cream missiles was a sign of the changed atmosphere. We were intent on leaving them no edge. The next day, Tuesday, I accompanied the two youngsters into downtown St. Augustine to the office of Justice of the Peace G. Marvin Grier, the hard-core racist who had acquitted the Klansmen who beat Dr. Hayling and his friends. He looked incredulous when I told him we were there to swear out arrest warrants against Herbert Manucy for assault with an ice-cream cone.

"You think throwin' a ice-cream cone is a crime?" he asked.

"It's assault and battery," I said.

"Boy, where did you go to law school?"

"Harvard."

"Didn't they teach you that you need a injury for assault?"

"No," I said, "assault is putting someone in apprehension of an unconsented-to touching, and a battery is an unconsented-to touching."

Grier paid no attention. He didn't care what the law was. But he did care that I had a big brother in Jacksonville named Bryan Simpson, so he finally agreed to issue a warrant charging Manucy with disorderly conduct.

In the evening, Al Bronstein and I met with James Kelly, the state trooper in charge of the state's investigation of civil rights matters in St. Augustine. Among other things, Kelly provided mug shots of a group of local hooligans which enabled one of our clients, James Hauser, to identify Herbert Manucy and four other white men who, on June 28 at the Fairchild plant where they all worked, had attacked and hospitalized him. Given the limits imposed on Kelly by his superiors, he was quite a decent man, sympathetic and cooperative with our efforts.

By Wednesday, August 12, testing at the restaurants and hotels was going smoothly with no denials of service. I began the work of wrapping up my stay in St. Augustine by preparing a series of memoranda and drafts of complaints on the matters I was leaving behind for the next group to carry forward in our tag-team litigation. Our court filings usually had the name of a Florida attorney on them, sometimes Earl Johnson in Jacksonville, and sometimes Tobias Simon, a prominent white civil rights lawyer in Miami. Murray Unger, a Daytona Beach attorney referred to me by Toby Simon, came to take over the Daytona Beach cases and some problems in Ocala.

In the afternoon, I drove to the Fairchild plant to pick up James Hauser to take him downtown to swear out warrants for the assault on him. As I pulled into the parking lot, there was Herbert Manucy harassing Hauser. I accompanied Hauser to the office of Magistrate Grier, before whom my welcome mat was wearing thin. Grier again balked at issuing a warrant for assault and battery, even though this time we could claim injuries. Now his excuse was that we had no witnesses. Finally, he agreed to issue a warrant, against a Manucy gang member named Coleman, for a "peace bond," meaning Coleman would have to post a money bond which he would forfeit if he again threatened Hauser. Grier's sense of law was Byzantine—at first he declined to issue the warrant because Hauser quoted Coleman as having said, "You will get your head beat in." Grier argued this was not a threat because it did not suggest that *Coleman* would beat Hauser's head in, whereupon Hauser remembered that Coleman had said, "I will beat your head in," and Grier issued the warrant.

While I was dealing with Grier, Al Bronstein was having a fruitful afternoon with Judge Simpson, who issued an order requiring equal treatment of blacks at Flagler Hospital. Judge Simpson was sympathetic to our inability to get the local police to protect African-Americans seeking service at public places, and said he would telephone the state attorney general. Al and I decided that, in addition to the disorderly charge I'd gotten the magistrate to issue against Herbert Manucy, we'd also file a petition with Judge Simpson to hold Manucy in contempt for the ice-cream incident.

My replacement, Paul Greenberg, an attorney from New Jersey, arrived in the late afternoon.

* * *

In the morning of my last day in St. Augustine, Thursday, August 13, Bronstein and I drove to the Fairchild plant and met with manager W. Hall and his assistant, Crouch. They had a well-developed explanation for their inaction in the attack on Hauser, which included supposed discrepancies in Hauser's story and a medical report indicating only a head abrasion. We let them know we thought it was a whitewash. I told them I had personally witnessed Herbert Manucy harassing Hauser in the Fairchild parking lot only yesterday. We said they'd better make sure their black employees were not bothered anymore.

In the afternoon, Al and I had an argument by telephone with Toby Simon, the Miami civil rights lawyer. Al and I wanted to schedule for the coming Monday the contempt actions against Manucy gang members who were still harassing blacks. This was the date Judge Simpson had suggested, and we wanted to maintain the momentum, the sense of day-to-day urgency. Simon insisted the hearings be later in the week so that he could be there, although his presence was not necessary, and finally said he would telephone Judge Simpson to ask for the later scheduling. We felt he was putting his own convenience ahead of the speed that would best serve the clients. It was one of several clashes we had with Simon in our short time there.

Later, I telephoned Judge Simpson to say goodbye. He praised our effort and the quality of our work. At five p.m., with some regret, I said goodbye to Dr. Hayling, got a ride to Jacksonville, and flew down to Miami for a weekend with my parents before returning to Washington.

Looking Back

In his Birmingham jail letter, Martin Luther King described the goal of his nonviolent protest movement:

[T]here is a type of . . . tension that is necessary for growth. Just as Socrates felt that it was necessary to create tension in the mind so that individuals could rise from the bondage of myths and half-truths . . . we must see the need of having nonviolent gadflies to create the kind of tension in society that will help men rise from the dark depths of prejudice and racism to the majestic heights of understanding and brotherhood.

That is exactly what happened to Judge Bryan Simpson. Near the end of my final visit with him, the Saturday before I left St. Augustine, Judge Simpson took out a file of what he ruefully called his "fan mail," hate-filled letters attacking him for his recent civil rights rulings. It was deeply painful to him to have become a pariah in his own community. But as the cases kept coming before him, he felt he had no choice. When the chips were down, this innately decent man was moved to take a stand.

In fact, the transformation experienced by Judge Simpson was universal. America was never the same after the summer of 1964. The country experienced a political and social revolution triumphant, without massive violence and bloodshed. Street protests and the American system of law were at their best, demonstrating their capacity to transmute the heat of the country's social struggles into courtroom battles, and, in doing so, to strengthen the nation. Racism and discrimination, although still endemic to this day, were dramatically diminished. The 1960s paved the way for the following decades which saw African-Americans capture the mayorship of New York City, the governorship of Virginia, and the top foreign policy positions of the federal government.

In the end, the civil rights struggle was a great healing for the country. And critical though they were, the law and the lawyers were only supporting players. The tension that gave rise to the changes was created by thousands of black people who physically and morally faced down the clubs, the fire hoses, and the dogs of hatred.

We changed too. Al Bronstein went home just to wind things up before returning as the director of LCDC's Southern operations. Richard Sobol—who had introduced me to Henry Schwarzschild and thus to St. Augustine—soon left our Washington law firm to become LCDC director in New Orleans. Before their years in the South were over, Sobol was arrested on a trumped-up charge and Bronstein was assaulted by a sheriff. But they endured, leaving a trail of legal victories. I left my law firm two years after St. Augustine to direct the Washington, D.C. ACLU. Sobol and I stayed in civil rights for over a decade, and Bronstein is still at it at this writing.

I like to think of the 1960s not as a lost Golden Age, but in the spirit of Dr. King's closing words to the eight white clergymen in his Birmingham jail letter:

I hope this letter finds you strong in the faith.

THE QUAKERS
1969

I n April of 1969, during the Vietnam War, I received a telephone call from Larry Scott, the leader of A Quaker Action Group, a segment of the American Society of Friends in Philadelphia. The police had told Scott that protest gatherings were not allowed at the Capitol, but the Quakers were prepared to engage in civil disobedience as part of their witnessing against the war. Scott asked me whether the Washington, D.C. chapter of the American Civil Liberties Union, of which I was now legal director, would represent any who might be arrested.

The ACLU's commitment to freedoms of speech and assembly had inspired it, sometimes at great cost in popularity and financial support, to assert those rights even on behalf of groups as loathsome as American Nazis and the Ku Klux Klan. Larry Scott's request presented a core ACLU case—citizens assembling at the seat of government to petition for a redress of grievances, an exercise of First Amendment rights—as the Supreme Court once put it, "in their most pristine and classic form."

The ACLU maintained a list of about two hundred attorneys in Washington, D.C., who stood ready to volunteer for ACLU cases without charge—lawyers in large law firms representing corporate and other business interests, sole or small-firm practitioners, academics, and law students. My job, as legal director, was to find a match for each case the ACLU undertook, a lawyer whose schedule, abilities, and preferences in civil liberties issues aligned with the case. I recruited a team of ten volunteer lawyers to deal with the Quaker cases.

The United States Capitol consists of a spacious center, 180 feet high, capped by a stately dome, and two wings, one extending north and housing the Senate, and the other extending south for the House of Representatives. The main entranceway to the building is up the long steps at the center of the east side of the building, sixty-five feet wide at their base. Security has turned the building into a virtual fortress today, but back then crowds of legislators, lobbyists, and tourists flowed over those steps every day. It was at the middle of those steps, for one afternoon a week, from late May through the summer of 1969, that the Philadelphia Friends clustered in groups of ten or fifteen and, in loud, clear voices, read from the Congressional Record the list of Americans killed in Vietnam. They were hard to miss.

The government was always on the alert in those years to stop antiwar demonstrations when it could, and promptly came up with an antiquated statute that prohibited "assemblages" on the Capitol grounds. This law had for generations been disregarded for most "assemblages" visiting the Capitol—students, Boy Scouts, Kiwanis clubs, religious and civic groups, and the like. However, when it came to protests against government policy, the United States Capitol Police were ready to enforce it.

Each afternoon weekly, that spring and summer, as the Quakers stood calmly reading aloud on the steps, James Powell, the chief of the Capitol Police, recited a prepared statement over a megaphone. Powell, a West Virginian who looked like a small-town sheriff, announced that, as custodian of the Capitol grounds, he was declaring the assemblage a violation of the statute and ordering those gathered to disperse. The chief warned that if they failed to do so they would be arrested. Each week, the Quakers quietly disregarded his order, submitted cooperatively to arrest and booking, and were transported to the cellblock of the District of Columbia Court of General Sessions, the local court, where they would wait their turn to be arraigned.

The courthouse, at 5th and E Streets, NW, was a three-story, rundown building in a rundown neighborhood. The lawyers who defended against the minor criminal charges over which the court had jurisdiction were the "Fifth Streeters," sole practitioners with humble offices in the area who were appointed by the court to represent indigents and who were dependent on the meager fees paid by the court for such services. Although some were good, the Fifth Streeters usually provided scant representation in a court dispensing assembly-line justice.

Courtroom 17 was where the usually sorry-looking lot arrested that day or the night before were paraded through arraignment—charged, appointed a lawyer, and fined, jailed, or released on bail pending trial. The Quakers were different from most who came through Courtroom 17—different from most antiwar protesters, for that matter. They were older people, nicely dressed, and dignified. Larry Scott himself was in his seventies, a tall, big-boned, big-chested man with a thick mane of white hair, a sort of beardless, gentile Moses.

Most of the Quakers arrested in the ensuing weeks were represented by our team of ACLU volunteer lawyers, but I handled the first three groups myself, to size matters up for a test case to challenge the constitutionality of the antiassembly statute.

* * *

The first group came down from Philadelphia on a Friday afternoon, May 23, 1969. Following the arrests, Larry Scott and I met outside Courtroom 17. We were admitted to the cellblock behind the courtroom where the ten Quakers who had been arrested were being kept, a barred area large enough to hold thirty or forty people. With their middle-class, clean-cut appearance and meditative demeanor, they lit up the usually dingy cell. Scott introduced me, and I proceeded to advise them of the charges and the likely penalty if they pleaded guilty, probably one to five days in jail or a fine of $25 to $50. I advised them that the ACLU would file a motion to dismiss the charges on constitutional grounds, and that, in the meantime, they should plead "not guilty," and we would ask the judge to release them on their "personal recognizance"—that is, without having to post bail.

Scott then said that the group had decided in their meeting house in Philadelphia that they would bear witness by engaging in civil disobedience, and, according to the principles of that practice, accept the punishment meted out by the court. Therefore, he said, everyone in the group was planning to plead guilty.

"Oh no," I said to the group. "Please don't do that. You're *not* guilty. The law they arrested you under violates the First Amendment. That's not a legal technicality. Freedom of speech goes to the heart of what human beings are about—our need and right to express ourselves."

They were hearing my gospel.

"The First Amendment is an embodiment of the basic spiritual values of our society," I continued. "That's why the Declaration of Independence states, *We hold these truths to be self-evident, that all men are created equal, that they are endowed by their Creator with certain unalienable rights, that among these are Life, Liberty and the pursuit of Happiness.*"

I paused.

"That's what the Bill of Rights is all about—rights that come with being human—with which we are endowed, *not* by a benign sovereign and *not* by social compact—but by our *Creator*. Freedom of speech is G-d given," I concluded. "We must bear witness to it, and not allow it to be desecrated."

Everyone pleaded not guilty.

The judge we came before, Tim Murphy, was a conservative and hard-nosed former prosecutor, but he saw that the antiassembly statute under which they were charged was questionable. Murphy promptly released them on their own recognizance pending trial.

Afterward, outside the courtroom, Larry Scott took me to one side. "Ralph, we are grateful to you and the ACLU for helping us. But with all due respect, you're a lawyer and you're talking to our people behind prison bars. In that setting you are throwing a lot of weight."

Of course I am. Isn't that my job, to steer my clients in the right direction? I thought.

Scott continued, "We admire your commitment to your beliefs. But we have a right, as Quakers, to meet in Philadelphia, and to reach our own decisions, based on *our* values, without getting down here only to have you turn everybody around. So when our people come here ready to commit civil disobedience and to plead guilty, while I respect the values you represent, please let us do our thing. Don't take unfair advantage of us. No more cellblock speeches, please."

Fortunately, the people who that day pleaded not guilty gave us the test cases we needed to challenge the antiassembly law. More to the point, I thought Larry Scott was right. I apologized and promised to sin no more.

* * *

It would be weeks before the ACLU's papers challenging the antiassembly law would be filed, heard, and decided. In the meantime, each Wednesday afternoon, the Philadelphia Quakers faithfully kept their date with Chief Powell on the Capitol steps.

The second group was arrested on Wednesday, May 28, 1969, and I represented them before Judge Alfred Burka. Burka was not a bad judge; he was not dim-witted like some of the judges, and not mean like others. But he was a lightweight who had gotten his appointment to the bench through his father's political connections—the old man owned a chain of liquor stores in D.C.

To appreciate Judge Burka's reactions when I appeared before him for the Quakers, we must go back to an encounter I'd had with him thirteen months earlier, in April 1968, a week after the assassination of Dr. Martin Luther King Jr.

On the Thursday of the assassination, April 4, 1968, riots broke out in several major areas in Washington, D.C. By five p.m., billows of smoke could be seen rising for miles along the corridors of 7th and 14th Streets, NW, and H Street, NE. Angry black crowds streamed through the streets, like a river overflowing its banks, looting and setting fire to shops, destroying everything in their paths. The mayor declared a curfew, and the police began making sweep arrests throughout these ghetto areas, gathering up everyone in sight, regardless of what they were doing, and charging them with disorderly conduct or curfew violation. In an effort to bring things under control, the government asked for, and the local judges imposed, a bail of $1,000, unusually high for such minor charges, and applied it across the board, without regard to individual circumstances. Naturally, no one could come up with that kind of money, and the thousands swept up in the next few days stayed in jail.

By late Friday afternoon, over 2,000 African-Americans were being held, and the ACLU realized that the judges were complicit in an informal, unannounced, and unlawful suspension of the Constitution, a kind of makeshift martial law. The national ACLU's Washington lobbyist, Larry Speiser, with whom I shared offices, helped me recruit several volunteers that weekend, and we hastily put together a federal lawsuit. By Tuesday morning, April 9, the number unlawfully held in jail had grown to over 4,000, and we filed the suit in the United States District Court for the District of Columbia. We sought a temporary restraining order to stop the sweep arrests and unlawful bail-setting, and to compel the release of those being held. The suit named as defendants Harold Greene, the chief judge of the D.C. Court of General Sessions, another dozen judges who had imposed the $1,000 bail, the chief of police, the U.S. Attorney, the U.S. Marshall, the city's Corporation Counsel, and the director of the city's Department of Corrections.

This challenge was received by the establishment with about as much good humor as one might imagine. The reaction began with Margaret Hummer, the U.S. District Court's motions clerk who arranged hearings before judges. This gatekeeper to the gods was a cold and haughty troll, and all lawyers with emergency motions in federal court had learned to kiss Ms. Hummer's ring if they needed to get before a judge quickly. Checking the papers I was filing to ensure they were in correct form, Ms. Hummer snorted her indignation and said, "This is the most outrageous suit I've ever seen."

It might be said in Ms. Hummer's defense that, for those few days, many people in Washington were frightened by the riots. But I was not in the mood for the customary bowing and scraping, and was apprehensive about being subverted by administrative shenanigans. "If there is any delay in our getting before a judge, we will file a formal complaint about it," I snapped.

We quickly got before Edward Curran, the chief judge, who just as quickly threw us out of court. A conservative and crusty old Irishman, Judge Curran listened calmly to the arguments presented by Larry Speiser and me. On the other side was Assistant United States Attorney Joseph Hannon, a bald and bullish man of about fifty, who bellowed in red-faced anger that he had not given up a leg in air combat over Germany in World War II to defend a country where a lawsuit like ours would be tolerated. Hannon sputtered that he was shocked that the "heretofore respected names of Larry Speiser and the ACLU would lend themselves to such a legal disgrace." I mentally noted with some satisfaction that he did not express shock that *my* name was associated with the suit. The facts, when they finally emerged a year later, in the form of a gently worded report of a judicial conference committee, supported the charges set forth in the ACLU suit. But Judge Curran felt no need to schedule a trial to determine the facts, or even to pause or reflect; he simply denied our motion and dismissed the suit.

By that evening, the riots had petered out, the fires were under control, and the authorities let everyone out of jail. We decided not to appeal. Maybe those jailed would have been freed just as fast without the ACLU lawsuit. It was just as well that we filed the suit without waiting to find out.

The *Washington Post*, which, like Judge Curran, had no need of facts to help it render a decision, editorially lambasted the ACLU for filing so "irresponsible" a suit, and Harold Greene, the local court's chief judge and the lead defendant in the case, denounced us in the press.

It was during the public furor over the ACLU's suit that

I received a call from Judge Alfred Burka, later to become the judge for the second group of Quakers arrested on the Capitol steps. In April 1968, when he telephoned me, I had never appeared before Burka, but we knew each other from the courthouse corridors and an occasional cocktail party.

"Was I named as a defendant in that lawsuit I've been reading about in the newspapers?" he heatedly demanded.

"You were, but you were in no way singled out," I said, trying to appease him. "We named as defendants all the General Sessions judges who for those few days sat on the riot cases. Our information was that all sitting judges participated in the setting of $1,000 bonds, which is what our suit is challenging."

"If that suit accuses me of violating anyone's rights, it's a damn lie, and I won't stand for it!" he shouted.

"Judge Burka, please don't be angry," I implored. "We're pretty sure that all the judges set $1,000 bonds in all these cases, but if we're wrong, that will be cleared up."

"You listen to me," he said, still not denying that he had engaged in the plainly preplanned and unlawful conspiracy to set uniform $1,000 bonds, "if you don't immediately dismiss me from that suit, I'll take you to the grievance committee."

"I wish you would not take this personally," I replied, still trying to mollify him. "We named as defendants all the judges sitting on these cases. Our suit is a test case, that's all. It's not meant to cast personal aspersions on anyone. It's a legal challenge to what was done. You know, that's what the ACLU exists for, to bring such legal challenges so the courts can decide what's legal and what's not."

"Don't give me that bull," he continued to fume. "You're just a bunch of publicity-seeking hounds."

That did it.

"Publicity-seeking hounds?" I said. "Look who's talking."

A few weeks earlier, Judge Burka had been quoted in the *Washington Post*, criticizing the ACLU's test lawsuits challenging laws treating alcoholism as a crime. He had questioned whether the ACLU really cared about the alcoholics it was representing in those suits, and contrasted our supposedly cold-hearted exploitation of them with the genuine human interest he showed by occasionally taking to lunch some of the chronic alcoholics who were repeatedly charged in his court.

"What are you talking about?" he asked with surprise.

"I'm talking about your posturing in the press," I said, "and your hair-brained take-an-alcoholic-to-lunch idea as a substitute for reforms in a legal system that abuses them."

"I don't see what's wrong in suggesting a little human interest," he said.

"Talk about publicity seeking," I retorted. "But that's beside the point. You've shown bad judgment in making this phone call. Now, in any case in which I appear that comes before you, I'll have to move to disqualify you."

"I wouldn't want to sit in any case in which you appear," he said.

"You won't have a choice," I parried. "This call has disqualified you. You are represented in this suit by the United States Attorney. If you have anything further to say to me about it, say it through your attorney."

On that note, we parted.

About six months later, in the fall of 1968, I had an opportunity to make peace with Judge Burka. Following the arrests of hundreds of antiwar demonstrators, they were brought for arraignment before several different judges. During a recess in my cases before Judge Harold Greene, I strolled across the corridor to watch a colleague, Phil Hirschkopf, representing his allotment of demonstrators before Judge Burka. There was a pause in the proceedings and, as Hirschkopf conferred with the prosecutor, I gestured a request to approach the bench, and the judge beckoned me forward with a smile. I leaned up to him across the bench, shook his hand, and whispered, "As far as I'm concerned, the past is water under the bridge; I'd be glad to appear before you if the occasion arises."

He returned my warmth with his handshake, and said, "I'd be glad to have you appear."

Having thus reconciled with Judge Burka, I had no reservations on that summer Wednesday in 1969 about appearing before him to represent the gentle Quakers. The marshals brought the Quakers into the courtroom from the cellblock and seated them in the jury box so that they would be at hand in a group as their cases were called, one at a time. The courtroom was crowded with spectators, including journalists covering the Quaker arrests. The first name was called, and a man from the Quaker group rose from the jury box and, escorted by a marshal, walked forward to stand before the judge. As he did so, I rose from my seat in the front of the courtroom and began to come forward through the short swinging doors into the well, the area in front of the judge's bench.

Judge Burka stopped me. "Just a moment, Mr. Temple," he said. "The court will determine who represents this gentleman."

"I represent him, Your Honor," I replied deferentially.

"The court will determine who represents him," repeated the judge. "Just have a seat."

Uh-oh, I thought. *What's this? Has the damned fool forgotten that we made up?*

"You are charged with unlawful entry upon the Capitol grounds, a misdemeanor," intoned the judge to the man standing before him. "You may plead guilty or not guilty, and you may be represented by an attorney. If you cannot afford an attorney, the court will appoint one to represent you."

"Mr. Temple represents me," responded the good Philadelphia Friend, whom I had never met.

I again rose, walked forward, and stood beside the man.

"If you are going to have Mr. Temple represent you," said Judge Burka, "the court will have to appoint cocounsel, because it is the experience of the court that Mr. Temple and the local ACLU are unprofessional and unethical and file false and irresponsible pleadings in court."

Oh, for heaven's sake, I thought. *He's lost it.*

A trial judge has great power over the lawyers who appear before him or her. There are literally dozens of discretionary rulings on procedure, evidence, and numerous other aspects of a case that are virtually nonappealable, not to mention those cases, both civil and criminal, in which the ultimate decision will be made, not by a jury, but by the judge. Even if a ruling can be appealed, most clients do not want or cannot afford an appeal. Lawyers, as a rule, will bend over backward to avoid antagonizing a judge, for it can damage the interests of the lawyer's present and future clients any time the he or she appears before that judge. My friend John Karr had to start transferring to other lawyers cases that got assigned to Judge Joseph M.F. Ryan, a malevolent alcoholic who did not hesitate to vent his prejudices in his rulings. In addition, judges have the power to hold a lawyer in contempt—indeed, to have the lawyer immediately locked up. As a result, judges are subjected for years to an unhealthy daily diet of lawyer kowtowing, with the toxic effect on some of evoking the arbitrary and peevish bully within.

As an ACLU staff lawyer, I was not dependent on my

practice for my livelihood, and most of my appearances were in test cases in which we and the clients were ready to appeal. This provided more room to maneuver.

"Your Honor," I said, "I move that those remarks be stricken from the record."

"Motion denied," said Judge Burka. "You know very well what I'm referring to."

"Your Honor, may I approach the bench?" I wanted to remind him of our courtroom reconciliation six months earlier. In any event, it was unseemly to wash laundry in open court.

"There's no need for you to come to the bench," he said. "You had no business naming me in that reckless lawsuit you filed during last year's riots. Those were lies and I told you those were lies!"

Great, I thought, *great timing, you imbecile.*

"Your Honor," I said, "the ACLU filed a test suit that was well founded. You took personal offense, and telephoned to threaten me. Under the circumstances, I move that you recuse yourself in this case."

"Denied," replied the judge. "There's no basis for recusal; this isn't a trial, it's only an arraignment."

"You're disqualified even for arraignment," I said. "I move that you be recused."

"Denied," he said. "Let's stop wasting time and get on with these arraignments."

"Your Honor, I renew my motion that you strike from the record your unwarranted statements."

"Denied. Now let's get on with it."

"Then I ask the Court to order that the court reporter provide an immediate transcript of this exchange."

"You don't need a court order to get a transcript, Mr. Temple," Judge Burka said. "You can order a transcript yourself."

"That will take two weeks," I responded. "I move that the Court order an immediate transcript so that I can be in the Court of Appeals this afternoon."

"All right, all right," said the judge. "Stop wasting time. The remarks are stricken. Now let's get on with these arraignments."

Judge Burka, a good man at heart, proceeded to release all the Quakers on their personal recognizance.

Having escaped a problem before the conservative Judge Murphy and the emotive Judge Burka, I was relieved the third week, as the marshals ushered the new group of thirteen Philadelphia Friends to the jury box, to see that we were before the wise, gentle, and moderately liberal chief judge, Harold Greene.

The first case was called, and Judge Greene and I ran through the litany of the arraignment process.

Then the judge departed from script.

Harold Greene was an exceptionally good judge but, like all of us, he bore particular imprints. As a young Jew, he and his family had been forced to flee Germany in the 1930s, after watching the Nazis undermine the democratic Weimar Republic with brutish rabble-rousing and violence in the streets. Judge Greene had a deep repugnance for disorder and lawbreaking, even in the form of nonviolent civil disobedience.

The judge asked the plainly unthreatening Quaker standing before him, "If the court releases you on your own recognizance pending trial, do you promise that you will not return to the Capitol grounds and engage in the same violation of the law?"

I said, "Your Honor, we do not believe there has been a violation of the law. The antiassembly statute is unconstitutional, and we will be filing a motion to dismiss the charges."

"Until your motion is filed, and until the court has ruled that the statute is unconstitutional," said Judge Greene, "the law is on the books and must be obeyed."

"Your Honor, may we approach the bench?" I asked.

"I see no need for that, Mr. Temple," responded the judge. "It is perfectly reasonable to ask for a promise not to violate the law."

"Please, Your Honor," I pressed, "it will only take a moment."

"Very well," said Judge Greene, with a sigh of impatient resignation.

With the Assistant United States Attorney, the court reporter, and me huddled at the bench, Judge Greene repeated in a whisper, "I don't understand what possible objection you could have to my asking them not to break the law as a condition of release."

"Your Honor," I whispered back, "these people are not likely to come back here. The Philadelphia Quaker group sponsoring these demonstrations is sending different people each week. But you are not going to get a factual answer from a Quaker to a question like that; you'll get a theological answer."

"I'm sorry," replied the judge, "I think it is reasonable to ask them to obey the law."

We returned to our places, and the judge once more asked whether the man standing before him would commit to not repeating the acts for which he had been arrested.

The Quaker responded, "If I am moved to bear witness against the war, I will do so wherever I am called upon to do it."

The judge said, "In that case, you will have to post bail, which is hereby set at $300." The man indicated he would not be making bail, and the marshal escorted him back to the cellblock, from which he would be transported at the end of the day to the D.C. Jail and held until trial, which would be weeks later.

The next name was called, and a woman stepped before the judge. With me standing beside her, the customary arraignment ritual was repeated, until we reached the bail question, at which point Judge Greene asked whether the woman would promise, if released, not to commit the same acts at the Capitol. I began again to ask the judge not to put the question, but was abruptly waved to silence. The woman replied that she could not make a commitment that might conflict with the call of Spirit. The Judge again set bail at $300, and this woman, too, was locked up. Judge Greene was visibly annoyed—annoyed at the Quakers, and, I was sure, annoyed at me.

"There is nothing wrong with asking the simple concession of obedience to law," he said, shaking his head at the unreasonableness of what he clearly felt was being imposed upon him.

The third Quaker was summoned and stepped forward. When the judge reached the problematic question, the woman replied, "I will hold the government in the light any place and any time that the Spirit moves me."

Judge Greene looked really upset.

"I am sorry," he said, "but we are a nation of laws. We all live under the same laws, and it is the rule of law that makes our freedoms possible. If everyone chooses to do whatever he believes regardless of the law, we have chaos, destruction, tyranny. We live in a democracy. If we believe that the government's laws or policies are wrong, we can vote the government out. It must be done in an election at the polls, not by disobedience of the law in the streets. We have an election, and then we must all abide by the results of the election. The majority decides. That's democracy."

The Quaker was a gray-haired woman of maybe sixty-five, tall, matronly, handsome—pure-bred Yankee. She returned Judge Greene's steady gaze and, in a calm but passionate voice, said, "I have traveled in the South and seen the bellies of babies swollen with hunger. And I have seen newspaper photographs of Vietnamese babies burned by napalm dropped by American planes. Napalm paid for with money that could be feeding all these babies."

Judge Greene sat glumly shaking his head.

"If this is what the majority wants," she concluded, "the majority is *wrong*. And I will bear witness against it." She took a deep breath. "With my body." Another breath. "And with my soul."

Judge Greene sat, still shaking his head, which now hung limply as he stared down at his bench-top. Finally he said, almost muttering, "Will you promise that if you are released without bail you will not engage in disruptive or violent behavior?"

"Yes," she answered.

"All right," said the judge, "you are released on your own recognizance pending trial."

The rest of the cases went smoothly. The only promise Judge Greene asked of the remaining Quakers was to refrain from disruption and violence, and they all promised and were all released, and the judge called back the first two and released them as well. Before the year was over, Judge Greene conducted a hearing on the ACLU's motion, after which he concluded that the antiassembly statute was unconstitutional as applied to orderly protest gatherings. That ruling opened up the Capitol steps to the tens of thousands of demonstrators that followed in the bright light cast by the Quakers that summer.

DESPERADO
1973

Lester Irby went on an armed robbery spree when he was twenty-six years old. He got to it honestly, so to speak, coming up in a ghetto of Washington, D.C., and compiling a typical record of juvenile offenses. But in 1973 he really cut loose.

Sally, now a lawyer for D.C.'s Public Defender Service, represented Irby when the law finally caught up with him. Sally was the consummate public defender, identifying completely with the bandits she was habitually assigned to represent, and usually succeeding in getting a jury or even a judge to also identify with them.

I knew I was hearing Sally's voice when, driving the carpool to school one morning, I heard my ten-year-old daughter telling another child about this great character, Lester Irby.

"He *shot* someone?" the other child asked in shock.

"Oh . . . he only nicked her," answered Kathy, shrugging it off and continuing her admiring account of her mother's favorite client.

Sixty-one-year-old Dorothy Roberts appeared to have been left none the worse for the wear when she told the *Washington Post* that she was sick and tired of having her small food market held up, so when Irby, accompanied by an accomplice, confronted her with a pistol one gentle spring night in 1973, she drew her gun out of a drawer and began firing.

"I don't even remember when I got hit," she told the *Post*. "I was shooting at him and he was shooting at me. My son kept saying, *Mama, please! Please, Mama, give him the money.*"

As luck would have it, a patrol car was cruising by at that moment, and the cops rushed in and grabbed Irby and his friend.

Given the seriousness of the crime, on top of the other armed robberies and his general criminal record, Irby was staring into the eye of a life sentence without parole. However, Sally, who believed that all her clients, no matter what their crimes, were salvageable human beings, persuaded Judge Harold Greene that Irby was not likely to be the same man when he reached middle-age, and won him a sentence of only twenty-five years to life.

Irby did not adapt well to prison life. In fact, in the beginning he did not adapt at all, escaping twice in the first six months of his imprisonment. As a result of those escapes (in one of which a guard was wounded by another prisoner), and a lot of talking back to guards who see their mission as the unrelenting dehumanization of their wards, Lester Irby compiled an early prison record that was . . . less than ideal.

His poor record for some years, however, only partially explains why his requests for parole have been denied, and why, as of this writing in 2002, at age fifty-five, he is still in after twenty-nine years of imprisonment. Once upon a time, people sentenced for crimes in which no one was killed or maimed were freed after ten or fifteen years. Lester Irby—or LT, as his friends call him—turned the corner and began using the prison programs to better himself and other prisoners after he reached middle age about ten years ago.

The real explanation for his continued imprisonment lies in the shift of public and political sentiment from rehabilitation to punishment, and the growth of a privatized prison industry which attempts to profit from imprisonment. This explains why the number of people held in federal and state penitentiaries in the United States has grown exponentially in the last twenty years, now up to almost two million.

My connection to LT might have ended when he was sentenced in 1974, or when Sally and I ended our twenty-one-year marriage in 1981. However, Sally kept corresponding with him until later that same year, when she passed him on to our then-sixteen-year-old son Johnny. In the years since then, Johnny has become a rock musician, a book publisher, and a constant friend of Lester Irby, writing and phoning him weekly and visiting him in prisons across the country.

In short, LT is an adopted member of our family. We think it long past time for him to be freed.

Imprisonment, which we employ promiscuously, should be a last resort, I believe, and those prison counselors who have worked most closely with LT for the past five years unanimously agree he is no threat to anyone. The only good reason for continuing to keep him in prison is that he is a writer, and I suppose it could be argued that we don't need more writers on the loose.

Sally, who always sent her clients birthday cards and had a way of bringing out the best in them, is the one who got LT writing. She asked him to write to her about his life and experiences. This produced a series of letters from Irby to Sally, sometimes addressing her as "Dear Shorty." They are as authentic a voice of Washington's 1970s ghetto as, say, Damon Runyon's characters were of 1940s Broadway, or Ring Lardner's or Mark Twain's of the lives and times of which they wrote.

Take, for example, these excerpts of LT's April 14, 1974, description of an Easter Sunday fight which he witnessed from one of the four storied tiers of cells surrounding an inside dining area in the Washington, D.C. jail. LT's grammar, spelling, and punctuation have mostly been preserved to keep the flavor:

> *A fight errupted in the dining area, between two guards and two inmates, that could have been a main attraction at Madison Square Garden. As I look on from my cell up above and the battle began to get heated, as every moment pass an added amount of pleasure enter my existance as the two inmates battle back to back and steadily took over command during the fistic affair. The dead-lock home crowd cheer on, and with every howling that came from their enthusiastic fans, the two in command dish out additional punishment to their noxious foe. I thought to myself "Black mama & White mama fights to the end." Yes, that's right, the two inmates are transvestites, but today they took off their dresses, did away with all their feminine ways and gave the enemies a boxing lesson I'm quite sure that neither one of them shall ever forget.*
>
> *Creamy is the one I referred to as "White mama." Although he is black his complexion is light enough to leave one in doubt, and his partner goes by the name of Jackie, "Black mama"— his ebony glows.*

LT describes how it started when two guards insisted on emptying the dining hall, and not allowing Jackie— "Black Mama"—to finish his Easter Sunday meal, even though he had only just gotten there, through no fault of his own. As the guards began beating the resisting Jackie, he struck back, encouraged by cries of support from the prisoners in the surrounding tiers of cells.

"Hit those bitches in their faces Jackie baby, both of um got just as much woman in m' as you" came another call.

The narrative then tells how Jackie's partner, Creamy, who had been leaving the dining area with the other prisoners to return to their cells, came running back, startling the guards and throwing them off Jackie. The guards got themselves together and charged back:

The guards started toward the pair. Creamy and Jackie step back a pace or two, and throw up their hands with their fist balled tight, and each processed a pose of a heavy weight Champion. Ah well, not heavy weights, but I certainly saw the styles of Sugar Ray Robinson and Carl Bo-Bo Olsen come back alive. It damn near shock the shit out of me when I seen the two guards knock back from a barrage of punches that Black mama & White mama served the pair. I would put up odds and bet it five to one that each of those two roller decided in their minds "Man, I have really put my hand in some shit this time."

I imagine all the rest of the prisoners were just as surprise as the guards of what was going on. As I say none of this actions ever comes from the homos, but during these times of various kinds of Liberations, one doesn't know what to expect. All human beings has the God given right to fight for what is theirs. And even if it was behind a few stolen minutes of a meal, aided with another siding with his companion cause, the two of them fought as tho the world was being taken away.

They grab chairs and whaled away at their foe, sending each one ducking and dodging. They slung food trays, threw salt shakers, tried picking up a dinning room table to toss that about. The two guards move around slipping and sliding, try-

ing desperately to avoid from getting hit, and the crowd roar on, "Get them stankin' motherfucker." I mean the house was really going wild.

LT reports that the guards finally managed to seize the two inmates:

Jackie and Creamy found themselves lock in bear hugs, each guard trying violently to press their foes to the ground. "Ow, ow, ow, Ohh, Ohh, ow, ow, the bitch is biting me." Jackie was chopping away on one of them. Perhaps my man should of let the gal finish eating her steak. Then came a cry from the other guard. Creamy had made him release his hold, and I saw him back tracking, holding his dick. Oh well, they said, you play, sometimes you gotta pay. And paying they did.

LT then describes how, seeing a squad of about ten riot-equipped guards enter the area and advance on the two prisoners, he uttered a silent prayer: *Lord, spare those two sissies from harm.* His account continues:

Well anyway, Shorty, I figure that the goon squad was going to jump on the two, but a thing happen today that off-seted the usual kind of scene. The kitchen crew gather around Jackie and Creamy as to show if necessary they would give them support. A beautiful happening because with the kitchen men available that quickly even the side, & with the sides even, at least temporarily no more hell would be raised.

Fortunately, Shorty, the confusion die down, Creamy and Jackie wisely choose to go down to the control center and talk the matter over with the Captain there in charge. This move avoided a bit of bloodshed.

Irby concludes his account with an observation:

Although I might of told you this story with a bit of humor, all that took place was of a serious matter. The prisoners and the correctional guards have a very long way before a understanding will come between the two. So many incidents start over very little things. But when one is living behind bars, all things become big, especially the few rights that a prisoner only have left.

Perhaps it wouldn't be all that bad if LT was freed. With two million prisoners, I guess we could spare a few, and maybe one more writer wouldn't hurt us that much.

SKOKIE MARCH—THE ACID TEST
1978

Letter to the Editor, The Washington Star, *February 28, 1978*

Your "Free Speech in Skokie" editorial (Feb. 9) argues that the American Civil Liberties Union and the courts have carried the principle of free speech too far in the case of the American Nazis' proposed march this coming April in Skokie, Illinois, a town in which 7,000 survivors of the Nazi holocaust of World War II now live.

The *Star* argues that the Nazis' virulent anti-Semitic and genocidal advocacy does not deserve the protection of the First Amendment. You suggest that the free speech principle was designed to protect speech, marches, and other advocacy only when they involve "valuable ideas," "ideas of conceivable truth, ideas deserving due consideration."

We strongly disagree. The right of free speech, including marches, is not designed to protect only acceptable speech, as the *Star* suggests. If freedom of speech were limited in that manner, it would be worthless.

Why? Because history teaches time and again that free speech is indivisible. As Yale's Professor Thomas Emmerson has observed, those in authority have an enormous impulse to restrict speech which challenges or attacks them or their policies. Thus, a right like free speech requires great societal discipline. It means putting up with all speech, no matter how obnoxious or ideologically destructive.

I fear that Lyndon Johnson would have considered much of the anti–Vietnam War movement to be the advocacy of ideas of no value. It took a series of ACLU cases to prevent the government from stopping antiwar demonstrations at the White House, the Capitol, the Pentagon, and other places. And what do you think Richard Nixon would have done with such a rule during Watergate?

The same is true of another rule that the *Star* would like to invoke to prevent the Nazis from marching in Skokie— namely, that "fighting words" are prohibited. The "fighting words" doctrine was pronounced by the Supreme Court in (and has consistently been confined to) face-to-face invective where a fistfight is likely to occur before there is sufficient time for the police to intervene to maintain order. A series of decisions, however, has made it clear that this doctrine has no application in the speech or march context. Otherwise, anyone could stop a speech he didn't want to hear.

Remember those days when Lyndon Johnson's secretary of defense, Robert McNamara, was hooted and howled off stage at college campuses because the audience viewed U.S. actions in Vietnam as genocidal and the speaker as a war criminal? Whatever one thought of the Vietnam War, it is clear that such a "heckler's veto" is incompatible with freedom of speech.

Think what else would happen if we devised a rule that certain kinds of speech, marches, or symbols could not be displayed because they were too arousing to the audience at which they were directed. Depending on who was on the board of censors assigned to administer such a rule, we might see Anita Bryant stopped from attempting to arouse public passions against homosexuals, or, if her faction was in power, we would see the advocates of homosexual rights muzzled.

Many of those who oppose abortions call the opposite view genocidal—could we rely upon them to permit advocacy of government funds for abortions? Should D.C. police have stopped the Jewish Defense League from demonstrating in front of the Hanafi Muslim house last year?

The process of law is one that develops a rule for one situation and then applies that rule in other situations. That is why the ACLU defended racist and anti-Semitic fanatics like Kunz in New York and Terminiello in Chicago in the 1940s. When blacks were arrested in Birmingham, in South Carolina, and in Chicago in the 1960s for leading civil rights demonstrations into white communities, it was the Kunz, Terminiello, and other similar cases that the Supreme Court relied upon and cited to reverse the convictions of the black demonstrations' leaders.

Freedom of speech is a rare principle in the world today. The United States is one of the only twenty-five countries, or fewer, of the 130 or so U.N. members that have freedom of speech. Not many nations in history have had it. That is because it demands a tremendous amount of restraint on the part of a society to confer certain rights, such as free speech, upon minorities, and to abide by those restraints no matter how strong the provocation to violate them.

I and others who have spent years studying the phenomenon of free speech are convinced of its indivisibility. Remember McCarthyism? That awful period of the 1950s occurred because public passion was aroused out of all proportions about the "Red Menace." The internment of Japanese-Americans in World War II is another instance in which community fears and emotions overcame the self-restraint that is vital to civil liberties.

The Nazi march in Skokie is the acid test of our commitment to civil liberties. Only by testing our societal restraint in the face of an exercise of free speech by the most loathsome among us can any of us be sure that, if the strength of public opinion should ever swing against one particular minority group, our fundamental rights would be secure. Ironic and painful though it may be, it is only by protecting the rights of the Nazis that the rest of us can feel secure that our rights will hold up if we ever really need them.

Recall the warning of Pastor Martin Niemoller: "In Germany, they first came for the Communists and I didn't speak up because I wasn't a Communist. Then they came for the Jews, and I didn't speak up because I wasn't a Jew . . . Then they came for the Catholics, and I didn't speak up because I was a Protestant. Then they came for me—and by that time no one was left to speak up."

Well, now they're "coming for" the Nazis. I am a Jew and I want to draw the line right there before they come for me.

Ralph J. Temple
Legal Director American Civil Liberties Union Fund of the National Capital Area

THE HOSTAGES
1979

T wenty-two years ago, I had a personal collision with one of the faithful of Islam. He was an Iranian, a Washington, D.C. rug dealer, and, as I later learned, and more to the point, he was the Ayatollah Khomeini's man in Washington. As my two companions and I followed him down the stairs leading to the basement of the large residence on that late Friday evening, I was entertaining both regrets and hopes. I regretted that I had not telephoned my wife, told her where I was going, and asked her to call the police if she hadn't heard from me by midnight. I hoped that if they bound and gagged us they wouldn't stuff rags in our mouths.

It was November 1979, and the Ayatollah's people were holding over fifty American hostages in the U.S. embassy in Tehran. It was not reassuring that when we had entered the Northwest Washington house a few minutes earlier, we found it barren of furniture, with assorted Muslim families sitting on the bare floors, making the place look like a refugee camp, or worse, a war camp.

It was less than two months before my planned return to private law practice after thirteen years as legal director of the local American Civil Liberties Union. With the children approaching college age, I needed to earn more.

Then, too, at forty-seven, I thought it was time to move on and make room for someone younger and less jaded.

The events that brought me to this ominous basement had begun that morning as I was driving to the office. I heard on the radio that President Jimmy Carter had banned a radical Iranian organization from demonstrating in front of the White House. The president said he feared that angry American crowds might attack them, and that televised reports might incite the radicals in Tehran to harm their American captives.

I groaned as I listened to the news. This was a gross violation of First Amendment principles, combining a classic "prior restraint" with a "heckler's veto"—that is, invoking a speculative apprehension that the speakers' opponents may physically assault them as a reason to prevent them from exercising their constitutional rights of free speech. For most of a decade and through the administrations of four presidents—Johnson, Nixon, Ford, and now Carter—an ACLU team of twenty volunteer lawyers and forty law students had beaten back the government's repeated efforts to stop demonstrations in front of the White House. The government's bans were driven by political rather than security considerations. In this instance, the White House's purpose was not so much to prevent harm to the hostages, as it was to prevent Jimmy Carter from looking any more impotent than he already did in the politically disastrous hostage crisis that would eventually cost him the 1980 election.

The ACLU's hard-won victories in preserving the White House as a place of protest were about to be demolished by a liberal president, acting in the desperate circumstance of the American hostages in Iran. Lawyers have a saying for that kind of dynamic: *Hard cases make bad law.*

The ACLU would sue to stop the government from in-terfering with White House demonstrations, but the ques-tion was one of timing. Would we sue right away, to try to enforce the right of the Iranians to march that week-end, or would we wait until weeks later, thus letting the government get away with suppressing free speech in the meantime?

I was dismayed to find that I did not have the stom-ach for an overnight lawsuit. We would have to be lucky enough to get before one of the relatively few federal judges who were committed to the First Amendment, rather than one of the many who were responsive to every government whining about order and safety. Even then, even if we suc-ceeded in getting a court order telling the government to allow the weekend demonstration, the government would immediately appeal to the United States Court of Appeals for the District of Columbia Circuit.

And there was the rub. That court consisted of nine judges, almost evenly divided between conservatives and liberals. The crucial swing vote and, I believed, the bell-wether for the court, was the dominant moderate, Judge Harold Leventhal. During my years with the ACLU, he was my litmus test of whether a civil liberties issue was worth litigating: as Leventhal would go, so would go the Court of Appeals. In 1975, when we won an eight-year battle, it was Judge Leventhal who had written the final opinion reject-ing the government's efforts to restrict demonstrations in front of the White House. This meant that, under routine policies of assigning judges to cases with which they were familiar, he was likely to be on the three-judge panel if the government had to appeal in this Iranian demonstration case. That should have been good news—but it wasn't. I thought that the government's invocation of the hostages' safety, although specious, would overwhelm the skittish

Harold Leventhal; he would cop out on this one.

I didn't want to make the crash-effort that was required by an immediate suit, nor, in such a futile effort, to sacrifice the weekend in the countryside that I was planning with my family and my cousin Sheila, visiting from London. The challenge could wait; we would bring it on a more civilized schedule, sometime in a month or so.

Arriving at the office, I put the matter out of my mind, until late morning when a young man telephoned.

"My name is Tom Munson," he said. "I'm a lawyer, and I'm outraged that the president has banned Iranian demonstrations in front of the White House. It's a flagrant violation of the First Amendment. I imagine the ACLU is working on filing a lawsuit immediately. I'm fresh out of law school and not yet admitted to the bar, so I don't have any experience. But I can help."

"Well," I said, "we'll get something going in the next month or so, and I'll get you involved in it."

"But the Iranian group was planning to demonstrate this weekend," he insisted. "Aren't you going to court right away?"

"Well, we can try to get something going in the next few weeks," I hedged, "but we can't really do anything right away; it takes time to put a lawsuit together."

"Why can't it be done right away? You can file a suit in the morning and ask for a temporary restraining order."

How did this young upstart get so smart? I wondered.

"We just can't move that fast," I lied. "Look, I'll take your number and as soon as we get things lined up, I'll bring you into it." I said goodbye and went back to work. Tom Munson telephoned again in the late afternoon, just as I was winding up and getting ready to leave. Once more I fended him off. My mind nattered about it on the drive home, but once there, I relaxed with my family and Sheila.

Two bourbons and a dinner later, about nine-thirty in the evening, Tom Munson telephoned me at home.

"Look," he said, "I'm sorry to impose on you, but this just isn't right. These people want to demonstrate at the White House this weekend. The ACLU should be filing a lawsuit right away, not in a few weeks. If I were admitted to practice, I'd do it myself. Why don't you get a member of the bar who'll stand up in court tomorrow, and I'll do all the work and put the papers together tonight?"

"You don't know how to do that," I said.

"No, but you can show me. I'll need some of your documents from another lawsuit to help me. But I'll get it done; I'll stay up all night if I have to. This is the First Amendment at the White House. We can't let them get away with it."

He was right, of course. *Good thing I'm leaving the ACLU,* I thought, *if the time has come when I need a neophyte to drive me into action. Oh well, there goes a beautiful weekend.*

"Okay," I said, "I'll make some calls and get back to you."

There were a handful of lawyers who might be willing to juggle their schedules to plunge into emergency litigation, but on a Friday evening I believed my best shot was my old friend John Karr. Karr, a couple of years and a hundred trials older than me, ran a small firm of three or four lawyers. When it came to a cause or a friend, Karr never said no.

When I got no answer at Karr's home, I called his young associate and close friend Will McLain, thinking Karr might be over there. "He's at a basketball game," Will said. "But, look, I'll work with you tonight. Let's just get the lawsuit together. You know Karr will go into court with it in the morning."

"Okay," I said. "Meet me at the ACLU office in twenty minutes. "We'll start pulling files and legal memos, and while you and Munson are typing up the documents, I'll get on the phone and enroll the Iranians."

I telephoned Munson, and a half an hour later he, Will McLain, and I met on the sidewalk outside the ACLU's office building at 6th and Pennsylvania Avenue, NE, six blocks from the U.S. Capitol.

Munson, in his midtwenties, was tall, broad-shouldered, and athletic looking. His conventional appearance, in a standard lawyer-suit, offset an intense and mildly wild aura. Will McLain, in his midthirties, was a blond Scotsman from Mississippi, a bespectacled and brilliant legal tactician. He and I were dressed casually in khakis and sweaters. We entered the ACLU's second-floor suite and began riffling through file drawers containing documents in similar cases. Will and Tom started ferreting out legal pleadings, motions, and research memoranda to use as models to draft, cut, and paste together the lawsuit and motions for an emergency order. We dreaded the long, slow hunt-and-peck typing job that lay ahead of us, but no one dared to risk losing a secretary by trying to draft one for this all-nighter.

While they searched, I telephoned my contact at the Iranian Student Association, with which the ACLU had worked before. I explained the lawsuit we wanted to file on their behalf.

"Not us," he replied. "We are not demonstrating now. With the hostage situation, the public is too antagonistic; it is not a good time. The group planning to demonstrate is the Iranian Revolutionary Council. They're *really* radical."

"Do you have a telephone number for them?" I asked.

He gave me a number, which I quickly dialed.

"Hello. Who calls?" asked a man with a guttural voice and a Middle Eastern accent.

"This is Ralph Temple," I said. "I am a lawyer with the American Civil Liberties Union. I want to talk to someone about offering the Iranian Revolutionary Council free legal assistance to keep the government from interfering with tomorrow's demonstration at the White House."

A pause.

"You must talk to Nahidian," he said.

"May I speak to him, please?"

"Wait."

Tom and Will were churning away at the documents.

After about three minutes, the same voice said, "Come here."

"You want us to come to your office?"

"To talk to Nahidian, come here."

"We are at our downtown office," I said, "working on the legal papers we need to help with the demonstration. It is difficult for us to come now. Can I just talk to him for a minute now, on the phone?"

"You must come here to talk to him," he answered.

The address was across town in a residential suburb in the northern peak of Washington, just off 16th Street, NW, about three minutes from my home where I'd just come from.

It seemed like a lot of running around when we were so crowded for time, but there wasn't much choice; we couldn't file a suit without a client. Given the priority of getting Nahidian on board, the three of us speedily hit the street, cramming the selected documents into our briefcases. Munson in his car, and Will and I in mine, headed west toward 15th Street, where we would turn north. It was now about a quarter to eleven. I hoped we could wind this up quickly, because at midnight I had to pick up my fifteen-year-old daughter at a friend's house, take her home, then rejoin Tom and Will at the office.

There was a time when such "ambulance chasing" was branded unethical. But in the 1960s the Supreme Court ruled that the Constitution protected the right of the NAACP to round up plaintiffs to challenge segregated schools in the South. Besides, the leading ethics scholar, Monroe Freedman, in his 1975 award-winning book on legal ethics, had declared war on a cluster of old ideas about lawyers' responsibilities. In a chapter entitled "The Professional Duty to Chase Ambulances," Freedman argued that it is a public service for lawyers to let people know their rights and to offer to represent them. He pointed out that the corporation that owns the truck that knocked down the man in the ambulance has plenty of lawyers to advise it, and insurance agents will be approaching the injury victim soon enough to induce a waiver or low settlement. Freedman contended that the profession *should* have lawyers out there earning a living by seeking out those who needed representation.

At the corner of 15th and K Streets, NW, while we were stopped at a red light, a woman in the skimpy shorts and blouse of her trade eyed us, then walked off the curb toward us. "Will," I nudged him, "here's our typist." Will grinned, but declined my suggestion and the hooker's solicitation.

We turned north on 15th Street.

We arrived at the same time as Tom Munson, a few minutes before eleven. The headquarters of the Iranian Revolutionary Council was a large home on a small street that ended in a cul-de-sac. As we strode up the front steps, the distances between the homes and the quietness of the street made the place feel uncomfortably remote.

We were admitted by an Iranian man, who asked us to wait. We stood embracing our protective briefcases as we took in the nakedness of the large foyer and living room, the whole encampment-like scene.

A new man approached us. "Yes?" he asked.

"We are here to speak to Mr. Nahidian," I said. "We just telephoned and were asked to come."

"Please follow me," said the dour man, in a tone more of command than invitation.

So there we were, apprehensively following our host down to the basement.

The basement, like the living room, was bare. The man beckoned, and three others appeared, set out chairs, and left. We sat, the three of us in a little arc, facing the somber Iranian.

"I am Bahram Nahidian," he said grimly. "What is it you want?"

I introduced myself and my two companions. There were no smiles or handshakes.

"The American Civil Liberties Union," I said, burrowing into the oppressive ambiance, "is an organization of people who believe the government must be stopped from violating people's constitutional rights. We protect the Constitution and the rule of law by suing the government."

Nahidian stared at me intently.

"We are here," I continued, "because we think the government is violating the rights of the Iranian Revolutionary Council by trying to stop the demonstration at the White House this weekend. We want to represent the Council and file a lawsuit tomorrow asking the federal court to order the government not to interfere. We are asking you to be our client."

"What is your connection to the U.S. government?" he asked.

"We have no connection to the government," I said. "The ACLU is an independent, private organization, funded by money donated by its members, thousands of people who believe in our principles of upholding the Constitution and controlling the government by legal action."

He appeared intrigued. "You are paid by this organization to do this work?"

"I am paid a salary," I said, "I and one other lawyer. But most of the work is done by lawyers who take time off from their work to donate their services to the ACLU because they believe it is an important cause. That's why Mr. McLain and Mr. Munson are here; they are unpaid volunteers. To us, the law and the Constitution are like a religious commitment."

The Iranian held up his hand for me to pause.

"Let me be sure I understand," he said. "You and your organization want to petition against your own government, in the American court, for us, the Iranian Revolutionary Council, because you believe they are breaking the law you believe in. And you do this for no fees, no money."

"That's it," I said. "Exactly right. Yes."

Bahram Nahidian sat back in his chair, holding his arms apart with open hands, and for the first time also opened his face in a broad smile.

"This is a wonderful thing!" he said.

With a light smile I nodded and said, "There are many wonderful things about America."

"I thank you and I respect you," he said. "This is a good thing you do. But this is not for us. We do not recognize any authority or law except G-d and the Koran. You speak of the American law. We do not care about the American law. We follow only the Koran. We are not interested in asking the American court for help."

"Sure," I responded, "I understand and respect that. But your devotion to the Koran is not necessarily inconsistent with your letting us represent you in court. The American police are under the American law."

He looked skeptical.

"Asking the American court to control their own police does not mean that you recognize the American court or law as higher than the Koran," I said.

He wasn't buying it. "There is only one law. We do not recognize your law."

At this critical, not to say precarious, moment, the youngest and least experienced member of our team spoke for the first time.

"That's ridiculous!" Tom Munson blurted out. "Your position doesn't make any sense."

Oh no, I thought to myself. *Tom, for G-d's sake, take it easy, we're in the den of a fanatic whose people in Tehran are already holding hostages.*

Nahidian's eyes widened. "What are you saying?" he demanded.

"You stop for red lights when you're driving, don't you?" Munson persisted. "That's not the Koran, that's American law. Of course you function under the law of the country you're in. Let's be sensible here."

Will McLain and I exchanged nervous glances as each of us intervened, trying to divert the dialogue away from Munson. It did no good, and Nahidian, warming to the conflict, answered him in kind.

"You have no knowledge of these things," he said, proceeding to demonstrate how lacking Munson was in good sense—something which at that moment, in the basement of the Iranian Revolutionary Council, needed no proof as far as McLain and I were concerned.

* * *

Midway through Somerset Maugham's novel *Cakes and Ale*, the protagonist says: "I wish now that I had not started to write this book in the first person singular. It is all very well when you can show yourself in an amiable or . . . heroic . . . light; but it is not so nice when you have to exhibit yourself as a plain damned fool."

This was just such a spot. It is still uncomfortable for me to remember my next action.

Having gotten McLain into that basement, instead of sticking with him, I saw that it was a quarter to twelve, and I announced: "Gentlemen, I do not mean to be impolite. Please forgive me, but I must leave now to meet my child and take her home." I asked Will to call me at home if we needed to do any further work that night, otherwise I would speak to him in the morning. With that, I beat a hasty retreat out of the basement, onto the street, and into the free, fresh air of the night, hastening to pick up my daughter.

The next morning, I telephoned Will to find out what had happened. He told me that Munson continued his verbal assaults, while Nahidian's escalating anger in that isolated place became more and more frightening. Will had finally managed to persuade Munson that it was time to leave.

"Temple, you son of a bitch," Will concluded in his Southern drawl, "don't you ever again get me down in a basement with two madmen and abandon me." I acknowledged he had a point.

Sheila, my family, and I enjoyed a lovely weekend in West Virginia.

As things worked out, a student at American University

contacted the ACLU the following week. He, too, had been incensed by the White House ban on Iran-related demonstrations. So he and a few friends formed "Students Opposed to Violence," calling for peaceful relations between Iran and the United States. He asked the ACLU to represent the group in applying for a permit to demonstrate in front of the White House, and, if it were denied, to file suit against the government.

In short, this sharp and gallant young man had constructed the perfect test case.

Our efforts to persuade the government to grant a demonstration permit were unsuccessful, and in early December we filed suit. Deputy Chief of Police Robert Klotz, who headed the D.C. Police Department's Civil Disturbance Unit, was honest enough when I cross-examined him to admit that no demonstration at the White House had ever gotten out of control, and that he believed his force could maintain order if Iranian-related demonstrations took place. U.S. District Court Judge Aubrey Robinson issued an order directing the government to grant the demonstration permit.

The government quickly appealed, we came before a three-judge panel of the U.S. Court of Appeals, and, yes, Judge Harold Leventhal was on the panel. The Court of Appeals reversed the District Court and ruled in favor of the government, allowing it to ban Iran-related demonstrations.

A few weeks later, on January 8, 1980, I returned to private practice, retiring from the ACLU.

Perhaps it is an unavoidable hazard of aging always to remember a supposedly better past. Still, I do yearn for that time when the militant faith of that Islamic extremist in the basement was met by an equally militant faith . . . in the American Constitution.

PART III

D.C. LIVING

A CHRISTMAS EVE GIFT
1981

The angels are in their appointed places,
Turn but a stone and ye stir a wing;
'Tis ye, 'tis your estranged faces
That miss the many splendored thing.
                    —Chinese, anonymous

It was Christmas Eve, 1981, about ten-thirty p.m., and I was home alone wrapping gifts when I realized that I did not have enough presents for my fifteen-year-old son Johnny. The next morning my wife Sally, from whom I'd been separated just over six months, would be coming over to join the kids and me. We had always tried to give Johnny and our seventeen-year-old daughter Kathy about the same number of presents, and here I was at this late hour a few short.

I jumped in the car and began to scour the town for an open shop. I cruised through Georgetown, down Wisconsin Avenue to M Street, then headed east to the downtown areas between 20th and 7th streets. No luck—Washington, D.C. was closed for the night. In desperation I headed up 14th street and finally discovered an open store, the enormous People's Drug store in the ghetto area of 14th Street just south of Thomas Circle. I found a parking spot on the north side of the circle, and, as I made my way to the store, politely fended off the colorful invitations of a horde of hookers.

This territory and the women plying their wares were familiar to me, as a few years earlier I would park around here and hike the fifteen blocks to my ACLU office at 14th and Pennsylvania Avenue. I'd learned then that it was best to avoid exchanges with the ladies. One dusk as I started for home I was sitting about the fourth car back at a traffic light just a half block off Thomas Circle, when a young black woman who may have been all of nineteen came up to the window of my car. Flashing a sunshine of an as-yet-unspoiled smile, she asked if I wanted "a date." I said, "No thank you, I'm a married man," to which she said, "Oh, I'll give you a better time than your wife, you don't really have a great time with your wife, do you?" to which I said, noticing that the light had just changed to green, and wishing that the cars in front of me would get going so I could drive out of there, "Yes, I do, really, we're just fine, really, thank you."

Now she escalated. "Oh no," she said, "not like me." I'm bobbing my head up and down in a yes motion, and just repeating, "Yes, yes, we're fine, really, yes." Beaming good humor, she replied, "Does she suck?" Car one has moved, then car two. *Come on, car three*, I think, *come on, come on, let's go, let's go*, all the while bobbing my head up and down and repeating, "Yes, yes, yes," and the car in front of me is finally moving. I start to pull forward, and she is saying, "Does she lick your ass?" and I, still nodding and repeating, "Yes, yes," finally pull away, as the girl, laughing, calls after me in her musical ghetto drawl, "You liiiiieeeee!"

I entered the drugstore as the minutes were speeding to

midnight. It was one of those drugstores that is more like a one-floor department store—it had everything. Cheap and low-grade, but ample. At this last minute before Christmas, with the clock running out, and the rest of the city closed up tight, the place was teeming with people. There must have been two hundred in the store, circulating the shelves, shopping, talking, laughing, and forming three endless lines at the cash registers. They were practically all African-American; I was one of maybe five white people in the store, including two of the half-dozen security guards. The joint was jumping.

I squirmed through the crowds and began scanning the shelves. As I was settling on a few items, out of the periphery of my hearing, I began picking up a verbal exchange that was turning angry. Then I heard a deep, bass, black man's voice say, with final and aggressive dismissiveness, "Das you're problem, not mine!"

The recipient of this dismissal, a short, skinny black guy, shuffled slowly past my back, muttering over his shoulder at the uniformed security guard who had just rebuffed his complaint. He muttered, "Das cute; real cute." A pause. "Only, you ain't cute." Another pause, as he continued to amble away. "You a great—big—fat—ugly—muthafucka."

Now the guard strode rapidly onto the scene, coming after the disgruntled speaker and into my field of vision. Suddenly, he was standing right beside me and glaring in rage at the customer who was slithering through the crowds toward the exit. The guard was huge, about six feet three inches tall, and, indeed, of intimidating girth. He stood there, enormous thick arms, hands on his hips, glaring at the skinny man, and bellowed threateningly, "What'd you say? What'd you say?"

By this time, my man had squirreled through the dense swarms at the cash register lines, and stood in the doorway to the street, one leg and half his body inside and the other leg and other half of his body outside. He stared back at the Dragon over the heads of the protective lines of people now separating them. Speaking slowly and with exaggerated precision, pausing between, and thrusting his head for emphasis of, each word, he said, "I say: You a great—big—fat—ugly—muthafucka."

With that he slipped deftly out the door into the night.

The guard, snorting with rage, suddenly turned and looked me dead in the eye. I had to exert the greatest effort to pull down the corners of my mouth, which had leapt up in a huge grin.

Christmas gifts can be found in all kinds of places.

THE TYRONE DEFENSE
1981

N ames are given to the stratagems in many fields of contest. Baseball, for example, has the squeeze-play, or the hit-and-run; football, the screen pass or the quarterback sneak; business, the leveraged buyout; chess, the Ruy Lopez.

Sometimes the tactic works, sometimes it doesn't.

The story is told that one night in 1913 the American chess master Frank Smith gazed even more intently at the chessboard over which he had been laboring for six hours. He thought he had uncovered a new counterattack against the Ruy Lopez. It is rare for anyone, even a master, to discover a chess maneuver that has never been seen before, but Smith, forging ahead, came to believe he had made such a discovery. Only five years earlier Smith had been defeated for the world championship by the great Cuban chess master Capablanca, using the Ruy Lopez. Smith spent the next six weeks exploring his new maneuver and researching all recorded championship matches, finally satisfying himself that no one had ever before used this response to the Ruy Lopez.

When a chess champion makes a breakthrough discovery, he does not use it right away; he saves it, preserves it, and waits for some special occasion before springing it on an unsuspecting opponent. In the meantime, the master cultivates his new weapon, practices it, develops its potential, hones it into something ever more overwhelming.

In 1927, Smith found himself again facing Capablanca in the final match, and had to choose between allowing the Ruy Lopez to proceed, for which Capablanca had made the initial moves, or making the simple pawn move that would force the game onto another track. Smith decided that this was the moment he had been waiting for, this was the time to unleash his secret weapon, and made the move that would permit Capablanca to proceed with the Ruy Lopez.

Years later, in his memoirs, Capablanca described the moment in roughly the following way: "I knew at once, of course, that something was wrong. Smith had not permitted anyone this opening since 1908 when I defeated him with it. I realized that he must have some new strategy, something he had discovered that no one had ever seen before, that he probably made this discovery years ago and had perhaps a long time to polish it into something devastating. I did not have to proceed with the Ruy Lopez; I could have diverted into a different attack. But I decided to accept the challenge."

Capablanca moved ahead with the Ruy Lopez, Smith counterattacked ferociously, and for the next seven moves Capablanca faced a succession of challenges, each of which required astonishing genius to avoid defeat. Capablanca overcame each onslaught, and went on to win the match and the championship.

That was an instance in which a combatant, Capablanca, relied on a generally powerful strategy which nearly failed because of a surprise opposing strategy. But the Tyrone Defense was nothing like the Ruy Lopez. The Tyrone Defense was used by public defenders in Washington, D.C., only because their indigent criminal defendants insisted upon it; the defense itself was an almost guaranteed loser. A classic model of the Tyrone Defense went like this: The defendant is accused of having mugged the victim on the street and run off with his wallet, the victim found a police cruiser up the street, the police arrested the nearby defendant, who met the victim's description of his assailant, and found on him the victim's wallet. The defendant claims mistaken identity, and that a passing friend had just shoved the wallet in his hand and asked the defendant to hold it for him. The friend's name? "Tyrone." Tyrone who? "I only know his first name." His address? "I only know him from the street." There were gradations and variations on this defense, but juries never bought it.

Well, almost never. I know of two cases where it succeeded. In 1968, I was appointed by the court to defend a man with a long criminal record named Alfred Player. The charge was that Player and two others, Tommy Trent and Bell Butler, had burglarized a lady's apartment in broad daylight and were then caught by the building janitor as they were carting a television set into a station wagon they had parked in the alley. The janitor, who, like the suspects, was black, shouted at them just as Player and Trent were loading the television into the rear of the vehicle. Thereupon, Butler, who was driving, tore the vehicle out of there and Player simultaneously dropped the television and leaped into the escaping car. The TV fell on Trent's foot and he dropped to the ground in pain, where the janitor sat on him until the police, called to the scene by a neighborhood kid at the janitor's bidding, came and arrested the man. In the meantime, Player, who knew the janitor and realized that the janitor had recognized him, told Butler after the car had gone a few blocks to stop and let him out. Player then returned to the scene and walked up to the janitor, who was standing there talking to two police officers, and said, "Bill, I want you to know that I had nothing to do with stealing anything. Bell Butler had told me that he's getting paid twenty dollars to move this lady's stuff, and said he'd give me five dollars if I'd help him." The Tyrone Defense. The cops immediately arrested Player.

When I interviewed him at the jail after I was appointed to represent him, Player insisted the story was true. He was walking down the street, the station wagon had come by with Butler driving and Trent with him, and Butler had asked him to help them move this lady's stuff. I asked him if he wanted me to try to negotiate a guilty plea, but he insisted he was innocent.

Sometimes when I would go into the ghettoes of Washington to interview witnesses, I would dress down—as in blue jeans and a shirt—so as to play down the "whitey" effect. In this instance I dressed up, dark suit, blue button-down shirt, conservative tie. I went to the building, found the janitor, introduced myself to him, and said something like: "Look, I've been ordered by the court to represent this man Player who," I sneered with skeptical disbelief, "says that he came back to the apartment and walked up to you and the police and claimed that he had been told by the driver, Bell Butler, that they were hired to move the stuff they were taking from the apartment. No one's going to believe that, but I have to ask you if he really did come back and tell you that—it's a lie, isn't it?"

The janitor answered angrily, "Ain't no lie—that's what he did—come back up and says to me that Butler told him that he'd been hired to move this lady's TV set and that he'd give Player five dollars to help him."

I said, displaying disbelief, "He actually came back and told you that?" and he answered with some aggression, "Yeah—that's what he said."

"You didn't believe him, did you?" I asked.

He snapped, "How do I know, how do you know? Yeah, I believed him."

The government brought Player and Trent to trial, but did not even attempt to find Butler, who my investigation found to have died in prison sometime after the crime in this case and before the trial. At the trial, the prosecution's main witness was the janitor who told of accosting Player and Trent while they were loading the TV set into the station wagon. At the assistant U.S. attorney's request the janitor pointed to the two defendants, identifying them as the men who were carrying off the TV. On cross-examination, I asked the janitor if it wasn't a fact that after the car had sped away, Player had not returned to the alley and walked up to him as he stood talking to the two police officers and told him that he, Player, had no knowledge that this was a theft, that he had been told by Butler that they had been hired to move the TV. The janitor confirmed that Player had done so.

I asked, "How close were you standing to Player when he made this statement?"

He answered, "About three feet."

I said, "Were you looking at him?"

"Yes."

"Were you looking into his eyes?"

"Yes."

Then I asked quickly, "Did you believe him?"

"Yes," he answered.

The prosecutor and the judge had become so absorbed in this interesting twist in the tale, that neither of them noticed that my last question was improper, because it is not relevant whether or not the janitor believed Player, whose credibility is for the jury and only the jury to decide. There was no objection. Indeed, so convincing was this Tyrone

Defense that Judge Oliver Gasch, a crusty old conservative and himself a former United States Attorney, granted a directed verdict without even letting the case go to the jury. Indeed, I had the impression that even John Terry, the assistant U.S. attorney in the case, a highly reputed prosecutor who subsequently became a judge on the District of Columbia Court of Appeals, was persuaded of Player's innocence. In the end, I think I was the only one who was sure that the cunning son of a bitch was guilty.

Of course, my use of the Tyrone Defense was rather manipulative. A much straighter and more aesthetically satisfying success was that of my former wife, Sally Brown, who was a public defender. In her case, the accused was caught red-handed by a policeman who, entering the accused's apartment with a search warrant, found the accused standing in his bedroom with a one-pound package of heroin on the bedside table. The charge was possession of unlawful drugs.

At trial, the officer testified to finding the defendant standing beside the drugs in his bedroom, and Sally asked him on cross-examination whether, in executing the search warrant, he had followed the rules and knocked on the accused's door before attempting to enter. "Yes." Did he announce that he was a police officer and that he had a search warrant? "Yes." Did he do so in a loud enough voice to be heard. "Definitely." Did he allow time for the accused to open the door before breaking it down. "Yes." How much time? "About a minute." No more questions, Your Honor.

Then came the defense. The defendant testified that he had lent his apartment to a friend, and that the friend must have left the drugs there, because he had no knowledge of them. He knew only the friend's first name and did not know where he lived. In short, the Tyrone Defense.

In her closing argument, Sally asked the jury: "Now, imagine: You are standing in your bedroom and you have on your bedside table a one-pound package of heroin, when you hear a loud knock on your door and a voice shouts, *Police, we have a search warrant!* If you knew you had heroin there, wouldn't you flush it down the toilet? Maybe you think one minute isn't long enough. Let me show you how long a minute is," and at this point Sally held up her watch before her eyes, and said, "Starting—now," and the courtroom was suddenly plunged into a silence which the reader may experience by suspending the reading of this account and sitting still until the second hand on her watch moves sixty seconds. The judge could not stand it more than twenty-five seconds, and interjected with impatience, "All right, Ms. Brown, you've made your point— let's get on with it."

The jury brought in a "not guilty" verdict in less than thirty minutes.

All in all, though, the Ruy Lopez is a better bet than the Tyrone Defense.

ME AND THE POPE
1990

I n the spring of 1990, I was summonsed to appear before a Tribunal of the Roman Catholic Church for the
Archdiocese of Washington, D.C. I'd already submitted an eleven-page, single-spaced narrative containing
some of the most significant and intimate details of my
life. The next step was for me to submit to an inquisition.

How is it, you may ask, that I, a Jew, living in a democratic society, should find myself in this situation?

My error, my heresy, was in preparing to marry a Catholic girl. The Church would permit her to continue receiving the Sacraments only if each of our prior marriages was
annulled. The Church rejects divorce because of a bibli-
cal passage or a fifth-century Council or something, one
of those millennia-old theological benders that outlives its
time. One night, my betrothed and I attended a meeting in
the basement of Holy Trinity with a dozen other previously
married couples to hear reform-minded priests and nuns
tell us how to qualify for Canonical annulment. It had the
feel of the church basement meeting where Father Barry,
the priest played by Karl Malden in the Marlon Brando
movie *On the Waterfront*, urges longshoremen to rebel against
their corrupt union.

The annulment spin was to make the case that our prior

marriages were doomed from the outset by reason of elements inherent in each of us. Of course, this is not a hard case to make for almost any marriage. As to my first marriage, twenty-one years and two outstanding offspring is really not a bad run. Even the parting had its successful moments. When I once remarked that my former wife had been generous in the division of our property, my daughter responded, "That's funny; that's what Mom said about you." Photos taken at the uncontested divorce hearing show my ex, her lawyer, the magistrate, and me, arm in arm, posing for and beaming at the camera.

But there you are. If the Church wants annulment, why fight City Hall? I painstakingly and honestly filled out the Church's application form, which called for descriptions of my family background, my school years, my personality and character, my ex-spouse's family background, school years, and personality and character, our courtship, the wedding, our married life and breakup, and the causes thereof. The document, dated December 12, 1989, concluded by asking the Tribunal to investigate my former marriage to see if it qualified for annulment.

The Tribunal, when I finally appeared before it, turned out to be the rather un-Torquemada-like Father Joseph Sadusky, a tall and lighthearted priest with a large belly overhanging his beltline, crammed in a tiny cluttered office of the Archdiocesan Pastoral Center on Eastern Avenue. He offered me a cup of coffee, put me at ease, asked me a few questions, and twenty minutes later sent me on my way.

The whole thing was sort of confessional in nature, like the scene in *Moonstruck* where Cher confesses, "Father, I have sinned: two times I used the name of the Lord in vain, I slept with the brother of the man I'm about to marry, and I bounced two checks, but I thought there was enough money in the account," to which the priest says, "It's not

a sin if you thought there was enough in the account—
but what was that second one?" and Cher says, "Sleeping
with the brother of the man I'm going to marry?" and the
priest says, "That's a big one, Edie; be careful, take care
of yourself."

I left Father Sadusky feeling somewhat relieved, if not
entirely absolved.

Driving my sweetheart to the Tribunal several weeks
later, my description of the easy time I'd had did not re-
lieve her stress, and as we pulled into the Pastoral parking
lot she began to cry. I burst into an adaptation of the "Officer Krupke" song from *West Side Story*:

Father Sadusky, annul it for me—
The marriage never really had a chance, you see,
Father Sadusky, don't leave us in the lurch,
We need the blessings of the Church.

Of the Church,
Of the Church,
Of the Roman Church,
We need the blessings of the Church.

She left the car laughing, the Tribunal recommended
the annulments, the Vatican agreed, and we got hitched
that summer and lived happily ever after.

THE KINDNESS OF STRANGERS
1991

"What happened to the bug?" my wife Sally asked me when she got home from the office. "Someone hit me on my way to work."

"Did you get his name and insurance company?" she asked.

"No," I said. "I was in a hurry and it's only a dent."

"Only a dent? The whole rear end is bashed in. We're lucky it didn't damage the engine." Volkswagen engines were in the back. "It's not like you not to get the guy's insurance and make a claim."

"It's just another dent; the car is fine," I said.

About fifteen years and one wife later, in the early 1990s, Ann and I went to a going-away party for the Rigbys, a couple very dear to us who were heading for the Philippines where John Rigby would run an international hunger organization and his efforts would win special recognition by a world awards group. At the party, we met John and Margaret Rupp, the parents of Megan, the woman the Rigbys' son Crispen would soon marry. So we were about to join families with the Rupps, so to speak.

"You probably don't remember," John Rupp said as we were introduced, "but we've met before."

Recognizing his name, I said, "Sure. You're a lawyer at Covington & Burling; we've never met face-to-face, but about twenty years ago we worked together by phone and mail on an ACLU lawsuit which you handled as a volunteer."

"Right," he said, "but we also met when I rear-ended your Volkswagen bug as Margaret and I were driving to work one morning in the late '70s."

"You were so nice about it," said Margaret. "John really smashed into you, and you immediately jumped out of your car and ran back to us and said, *Are you okay?*"

John continued, "I said, *Yes, we're all right; are you all right?* You obviously didn't know who I was, but you said, *I'm okay . . . you're okay . . . let's forget it . . . okay?* and I said, *Sure*, and you said, *Okay*, and jumped back in your car and took off."

Margaret Rupp then added, "I said to John, *Wasn't that Ralph Temple?* and he said yes, and I said, *What a nice guy; you really bashed in the rear end of his car, and he just says, 'Let's forget it.'*"

"Yes," concluded John, "that was really generous of you."

I sipped my bourbon.

"Not entirely," I said. "In those years, I never smoked during the day, but on that particular morning, we had just finished a mammoth job on a brief and gotten it filed, and I was driving into the office free as a lark with no hovering deadlines, and, in my exhilaration, celebrated by lighting up a joint."

The Rupps looked startled.

"Gliding down 16th Street, as I passed Carter Barron, I spotted someone I knew waiting at a bus stop. I had just gone by him, but I started to brake thinking I'd give him a ride, but then I thought, *No, I've gone too far past him,* and began to accelerate again, and then I thought, *No, I'm not too far past him,* so I started to brake again, when I thought,

Wait a minute—the car is full of fumes, and was getting ready to accelerate again, when . . . *WHAM!* Thoughts came quickly: *Rear-ended . . . exchange names and insurance information . . . holding up rush-hour traffic . . . cops . . . the car is full of fumes . . .* I jump out and run back and say, *Are you okay?* and you say, *Yes,* and I say, *You're okay . . . I'm okay, you're okay . . . let's forget it . . .* I'm outta here."

It was a good party, and we liked the Rupps. I think they forgave my having deprived them of a fond memory of a forgiving stranger.

PART IV

TEMPLE ON CLINTON

IMPEACH HIM? NO, GET REAL
1997

Originally published in the Oregonian, *December 17, 1997*

C ensuring or otherwise punishing the president is a bad idea. It is far more corrupting of our cultural and moral values to punish Bill Clinton, and thus legitimize the political manipulations and violations of sexual privacy that have taken place, than any supposed harm from the president's sexual conduct or evasions. Privacy, and other rights at the core of what it means to be a free and autonomous individual in a democratic nation, are vital moral principles of our national life. Allowing and exploiting the violation of those rights is as morally degenerating to our society as any violation of the Ten Commandments. I'm not condoning the president's actions, but denunciations of him reflect a failure to appreciate the enormity of the violations of fairness and privacy that were committed.

The American people know this, which is why the year-long inflammatory disclosures and negative publicity have not only failed to shake public support for the president, but have increased it.

Unlike the president's critics, the public appreciates the fact that it is societally unhealthy and morally wrong to use the knowledge of what is legitimately private, gained by wrongful exposure, to condemn and demean the one whose privacy is violated. Not that disclosures obtained in violation of privacy should always be disregarded. The seriousness of the disclosures as a matter of public concern must be weighed against the seriousness of the intrusions on privacy. In this case, the sexual conduct and evasions to conceal it, including the alleged perjury, have relatively little bearing on the public interest, whereas the privacy violations strike at the heart of the public interest . . .

All who value privacy rights should align themselves with the public's values. And Republicans and the media should note that if they continue to fail to embrace those values they will remain where they have been all year—alienated from the people.

CONSPIRACY, MORALITY, AND THE MEDIA
1998

Originally published in the Ashland Daily Tidings, *March 11, 1998*

The real scandal in the Monica Lewinsky affair is that there is a right-wing conspiracy behind the effort to destroy the president, and the mainstream media are primary coconspirators.

The law of conspiracy does not require that the participants hatch the plan around a backroom table. Participants can join the conspiracy as it develops, and it is enough that each is aware of the others and knows that each will do his part—all committed to the common purpose of the conspiracy. In an antitrust conspiracy, businesses act, seemingly one by one, to raise or lower prices, each knowing that the others will follow suit, and all doing it with the knowledge that they act in concert for a common goal. Same thing in a drug conspiracy. Same thing is the Monica Lewinsky case.

Senator Helms got his protégé, federal Judge David Sentelle, to appoint Kenneth Starr. After several years of unsuccessful efforts to find criminal conduct by President Clinton, Starr was fed the Lewinsky tapes by Linda Tripp, prompted by Lucianne Goldberg, George Conway, and James Moody. Except for the hapless Ms. Lewinsky, they are rabid right-wingers, every one of them, each acting with the knowledge of what the others will do, with the common goal of bringing down the Clinton presidency.

The media's conscious participation in the conspiracy is evidenced, among other things, by their use of illegal leaks by Starr to circulate stories lacking supporting evidence. From the outset, the mainstream media predicted that the president would face resignation or impeachment—a suggestion so farfetched as itself to add evidentiary support of conspiracy. Of course, the media did not say that they wanted to see the president removed—only that the public would demand it as more facts emerged.

The president quite naturally kept attending to the affairs of state, delivering a powerful report on the state of the union. The media suggested it was the president's strategy to divert public attention from the Lewinsky scandal to Social Security, the economy, the poor, and Iraq. Imagine.

The media may be forgiven their shock at discovering their inability to deliver on their part of the conspiracy. After all, everything ultimately depends on the media's bringing the public along. And crueler shock yet: the public is accusing the media of recklessness, of immorality, of detestable conduct.

The media initially responded by whining that the public had sold out for economic prosperity, which it credited to the president. The *New York Times* also sounded a more hopeful notion—that the president did not understand "the metabolism of a long-running Washington story," that, as more facts came out, day after day, the public would turn against the president. It rang like the media's redeclaration of war: *We'll keep this thing front page for as long as it takes.*

But the public still was not buying. Next, CBS and the *Times* happily noted that although the latest poll showed only 7 percent of the public was really interested in the story, 25 percent said they thought that others were really into it. This, the media urged, shows that the public is in denial, is lying to itself, that the public really is concerned and eventually will turn against the president.

By mid-February, the public's continuing support of the president and its increasing revulsion at the media had forced the subject off the front page and reduced the media to trying to manufacture a rift between the president and his confidantes, and to gloating about Clinton's exclusion from "the Washington establishment"—the foundering gasps of the faltering conspiracy.

The public is not in denial, and it has not sold out. The public is trying to let the media know that there is greater moral value and a healthier political and social atmosphere in not losing ourselves in the sex lives of our leaders; that respect for a minimal level of privacy is itself an important moral value.

The media, which understood this in the times of Roosevelt, Eisenhower, Kennedy, and Dr. Martin Luther King Jr., nonetheless have promoted sex as a political issue over the last thirty years, and of course greeted the invitation to join the Starr conspiracy with a frenzied wallowing in the concocted lascivious details. Mr. Starr had every reason to count on the media, and they have come through—egging him on in his increasingly despicable antics.

Someone is in denial, and it is not the public. Someone is debasing our moral, political, and cultural lives, and it is not the president. No wonder Morton Kondracke, editor of Capitol Hill's *Roll Call*, in his 1994 Catholic University commencement address, named the media as the most destructive institution in American today.

CLINTON INNOCENT, GOP GUILTY
1999

Originally published in the Ashland Daily Tidings, *March 12, 1999*

N ow that the president has been acquitted, what is the moral state of America? Outrage is dead, cries William Bennett, the great Republican moralist. No it's not, Mr. Bennett, it's aimed at you and your colleagues.

Never have the American people more honorably conducted themselves than in their unwavering support of President Clinton in the teeth of an extended right-wing and media campaign to destroy his presidency. Americans know that private, consensual sexual misdeeds are not nearly as harmful to our moral, cultural, and political life as the abusive right-wing conspiracy led by Kenneth Starr and supported by an all-too-willing media, that attempted to set the president up for impeachment on perjury and obstruction of justice charges.

Even if the president had lied, his public support is fully warranted, because his private, consensual sexual conduct is no one's business but his family's. The public reacted similarly when it learned that J. Edgar Hoover tape-recorded Dr. Martin Luther King Jr.'s adulterous encounters; Hoover was scorned, and Dr. King's private conduct has been forgiven and forgotten, as he continues to be honored for his moral leadership.

The fact is, the president is not guilty of the impeachment charges, for there is no evidence of perjury or obstruction. The House Republicans' case is based on inferences and assumptions that are refuted by direct testimony and evidence.

The Perjury Charge

The president told the truth to the grand jury. He admitted that he had "inappropriate intimate" contacts with Ms. Lewinsky, and quite properly refused to provide more detail. When asked before the grand jury whether he told the truth in the Paula Jones deposition, Mr. Clinton said he tried to stay within the strict limits of the truth while being as unhelpful as possible. This was a truthful answer, since he considered in the Jones deposition that oral sex is not "sexual relations," a definition shared by most college students according to a legal study. The president was not charged with perjury in the Jones deposition. Thus, while the president, as he has acknowledged, misled the public, he did not commit perjury.

Obstruction of Justice Charge

The president is charged with trying to induce Ms. Lewinsky to lie in the Paula Jones case, trying to get her a job as an inducement to lie, and taking back his gifts to conceal evidence. But Ms. Lewinsky testified to the contrary, as did the president's secretary, Betty Currie, who said that she recovered the gifts at Ms. Lewinsky's request without the president's involvement. The president is also charged with pressuring Ms. Currie to lie in the Jones case by saying to her, "You were always there when Monica was there, we were never really alone, Monica came on to me, and I never touched her, right?" But Ms. Currie testified that the president was just giving his version, that she felt no pressure, and that she told him her recollection differed from his. It is clear that the president's effort to mislead Ms. Currie, like similar efforts with other staff members, was aimed not at the Paula Jones case, in which none of them was a witness, but at the media storm about the Lewinsky affair that he was expecting after his Jones case deposition. There is no evidence of obstruction of justice.

The president is guilty of only private sins. It is Ken Starr, the Republicans, and the mainstream media that have violated the public trust and are deserving of censure. Even Reagan-conservative journalist Andrew Sullivan has denounced the campaign against the president, writing in the *New York Times* that "truly American conservatives wouldn't have shredded the virtues of privacy and decency and common sense for the emotional release of a cultural jihad."

The Republicans continue to wallow in the impeachment swamp, while the president busies himself serving the nation by pressing for peace in the world's hotspots, containing Saddam Hussein, and promoting vital domestic programs. The public, meanwhile, has named President Clinton as the most admired person of 1998, and censured the Republicans where it counts—at the ballot box.

Congratulations to the American people for directing their moral outrage at the right targets.

Ralph J. Temple
150 Meyer Creek Road
Ashland, OR 97520
(541) 482-9868

April 14, 2000

Richard Gephardt
U.S. House of Representatives

Dear Congressman Gephardt:

Your fundraising cover letter (encl.) is correct: I am a "good and loyal friend" of the Democratic Party.

But you are not.

You deserted Bill Clinton and the Democratic Party at the earliest, and what must have appeared to you, the most opportunistic moment.

When the president was under intense fire by this tawdry group of right-wing fanatics—with the flames fanned by a national media that has joined in that attack from the beginning of the Clinton administration— you were the first important Democrat in the House, joining that pious fool Lieberman in the Senate, to jump ship, give aid and comfort to that misbegotten bunch of Republicans in the House, and joining in the spurious attack on our president over an act of sexual misconduct.

That action betrayed a weakness of character and courage on your part, in the opinion of tens of thousands of us.

Of course, you saw right quick that the public was not going to join in the stoning of someone for adultery, so you switched back to the right horse—which you should have stayed with in the first place.

And so, fair-weather friend, Bill Clinton may have forgiven you, but we haven't.

I wouldn't vote for you for dog-catcher.

And the Democratic Party would do better not to have your name on its fundraising appeals. Like many other Democrats, I respond with a contribution to just about every Democrat fundraising letter I get— except yours.

Ralph Temple

PART V

THE NEW MILLENNIUM

THE MEDIA'S COP-OUT ON THE APRIL DEMONSTRATIONS

2000

Letter to the Editor, The Washington Post, *August 16, 2000*

"Hail to the Chief and His Cops," began the *Washington Post*'s April 19 editorial, leading a chorus of media praise for the Washington, D.C. police response to demonstrations against the world trade organizations.

A few weeks ago, however, the American Civil Liberties Union, in a federal class-action lawsuit, charged that the police violated rights of speech and assembly by sweep arrests and dispersals of orderly demonstrators, assaulting many with clubs and gas, detaining those arrested for excessive periods under harsh and unlawful conditions, and preemptively closing the demonstrators' headquarters and seizing political materials.

The events were witnessed and filmed by journalists, so there is no real question that the police acted as charged. Nor is there much question that these police actions, commended by the press for their efficiency, were unlawful. That was established a generation ago when this same police force indulged in the same sweep-the-street tactics against antiwar protesters. The ACLU then, as now, filed federal lawsuits. The Washington, D.C. police then,

as now, defended such measures as necessary to keep traffic flowing and buildings open. The media then, as now,
lavished unrestrained praise on the police.

The federal courts responded differently. Citing long-
standing principles of constitutional law, the courts told
the police in the 1970s case that their job was to maintain
clear passage, not to sweep orderly demonstrators off the
streets. As one federal court put it: "The police may not
simply claim exasperation at the enormity of the task and
defer constitutional rights to convenience." The federal
courts condemned the D.C. police actions as unconstitutional, called upon them to conform their methods to the
law, and assessed millions of dollars in damages.

The first time since then that the D.C. police were
tested on their ability to act lawfully while controlling mass
protests was April 2000. During the intervening decades,
Washington has seen no mass *protest* demonstrations. The
Million Man March and the scores of gatherings since then
have been in the nature of huge meetings, always carefully
orchestrated with the full cooperation of the government.
In dealing with the April protests, the government chose
to repeat the very police methods that have been declared
unlawful. And once again the government has the media's
blessings for abusing the First Amendment.

As media scholar Robert McChesney has observed,
journalism is at its worst in those matters in which the political and economic establishments and the government
are aligned. The hostility of those institutions to mass protest demonstrations, in general, and to the antiglobalization
movement, in particular, proved too daunting a challenge
to journalistic objectivity. The result is an uncritical press
response to police actions that do violence to the demonstrators and to the First Amendment.

This is a grave mistake. Allegiance to our Constitution

has been one of America's great national strengths. We have been able to incorporate within our political system great tides of discontent without the widespread and ongoing violence suffered by other nations, even Great Britain. It was our commitment to a Constitution that is historically unique in the protection it affords political and ethnic minorities that enabled us to transmute the civil rights and antiwar movements into great social and political change without the breakdown of law. Street protests protected by the First Amendment played a crucial part. In the promises and hazards of the next few decades of great national and global change, we should be cautious not to lose that tradition by failing to honor it.

The media must do better. A good start would be to apply the same critical journalistic and editorial vigor to police actions in demonstrations as is usually reserved for sex and money scandals. It is time for the media to enter this arena with the determination to fulfill its Fourth Estate role as a major guardian of the First Amendment.

THE SORROW AND THE PITY
OF RACIAL PROFILING
2001

Originally published in It's a Free Country: Personal Freedom
in America After September 11 *(RDV/Akashic Books, 2002)*

I f Jewish extremists, like Yigal Amir who assassinated
Israeli Prime Minister Yitzakh Rabin in 1995, ever
engaged in acts of terrorism in the United States, a
roundup of foreign Jews would be likely to follow. There is
an echo of lynchings and pogroms in the indiscriminate arrests of over 1,100 Middle Eastern men following the September 11 terrorist attacks. Such raids are an atavistic yet
time-honored response. The dragnet of Arabs and Muslims
has not yielded results, any more than did the 1920 Palmer
raids, the 1940s internment of Japanese-Americans, or the
1979 crackdown on Iranians during the hostage crisis. But
the roundups reassure the public.

For Muhammad Rafiq Butt, a fifty-five-year-old working-
class Pakistani free of any links to terrorism whose only offense was an expired visa, the experience meant death. The
first fatality of the racial profiling of Arabs and Muslims following the September 11 attacks, Butt, arrested by the FBI,
died of a heart attack after languishing for thirty-three days
in a New Jersey county jail. In *The Gulag Archipelago*, Alek-
sandr Solzhenitsyn characterizes that experience:

Arrest! Need it be said that it is a breaking point in your life, a bolt of lightning which has scored a direct hit on you? That it is an unassimilable spiritual earthquake not every person can cope with . . .

Many other accounts of broken lives have emerged from the sweep arrests, and as of this writing nine months later, hundreds are still being held. The arrests were followed by the Justice Department's program to interrogate another 5,000 Arabs and Muslims, and in March 2002 several thousand more were added to the interrogation list. In June 2002 the department announced that it planned to fingerprint and photograph an additional 100,000. Middle Eastern people boarding airliners are being specially screened, and harassed.

The public, identifying with the 3,000 murdered in the September 11 attacks, has not concerned itself much with the implications of this broadscale targeting of an ethnic minority. Bombarded on our own soil for the first time in two centuries, Americans are desperately afraid that one of us may be next—on an airliner, in a building, on the street. The traumatized political atmosphere has encouraged a vast expansion of government powers at the expense of traditional rights, and is reflected most dramatically in the public's embrace of racial profiling of Muslims.

Some liberals have joined the stampede. Journalist Michael Kinsley, in a September 30, 2001, article in the *Washington Post*, argues, "[T]oday we're at war with a terror network that just killed 6,000 innocents and has anonymous agents in our country planning more slaughter. Are we really supposed to ignore the one identifiable fact we know about them? That may be asking too much."

Kinsley reasons that "an Arab-looking man heading

toward a plane is statistically more likely to be a terrorist." Stuart Taylor Jr., in the conservative *National Journal*, similarly invokes "statistics," arguing that "100 percent of the people who have hijacked airliners for the purpose of mass-murdering Americans have been Arab men." These arguments have no basis in the science of statistics. Statistical validity requires more than the likelihood that the suspect is of one race rather than another; it requires that the selected group contains a sufficient probability of return to justify the selection. As these pundits acknowledge, the statistical yield of terrorists from screening all young Arab men is likely to be "tiny" or "infinitesimal."

The very occurrence of September 11 demonstrated the profound incompetence of the FBI, the CIA, and the Immigration and Naturalization Service (INS). Yet America, in denial, seems incapable even now of facing the extent to which years of spectacular bungling by these agencies has left us dangerously exposed. The ethnicity, age, and sex were in fact not the "one identifiable fact" known about the nineteen September 11 terrorists. Some were already on watchlists but were missed anyway, while the conduct of others should have aroused suspicions. Even six months after the attacks, the INS unwittingly extended the visas of two of the dead September 11 terrorists. Congress has responded to the colossal failures of the FBI and the CIA by throwing more money into their already bloated budgets. The country thus reaches not for real security but for the habitual bromide of racial profiling, which diffuses and squanders investigative resources, undermining rather than enhancing public safety. Racial profiling is invoked, not for any proven effectiveness nor for lack of more sharply focused alternatives, but as a pacifier for a frightened public.

The notion that all members of the perpetrators' race or

ethnic group are suspect, and therefore may be separated out for special treatment, has a familiar ring from an earlier era:

> [W]e cannot reject as unfounded the judgment . . . that there were disloyal members of that population whose number and strength could not be precisely and quickly ascertained. We cannot say that the . . . government did not have ground for believing that in a critical hour such persons could not readily be isolated and separately dealt with, and constituted a menace to the national defense and safety . . .

So did the Supreme Court, in *Korematsu vs. United States*, justify the World War II evacuation into concentration camps of 120,000 Japanese-Americans, an action for which the nation later confessed error and paid reparations. It is an all-too-common reaction to regard with fear and hostility all those of another racial or ethnic group. Civility and decency, not to say our genuine safety, frequently demand that we rise above our reactive fears and inclinations. That is in large part the function in a society of the rule of law.

The Rule of Law

The Constitution was intended to limit the public's misguided passions against individuals and minorities by defining certain rights that are intrinsic. As Jefferson expressed it in the opening lines of the Declaration of Independence: "We hold these truths to be self-evident, that all men are created equal, that they are endowed by their Creator with certain unalienable rights, that among these are Life, Liberty and the pursuit of Happiness."

Civil liberties are the gift, the endowment, given us by "the Creator," not by the ACLU, not by the happenstance of "legal technicalities," not even by the Founding Fathers or

John Locke's social compact. In short, and in less sectarian terms, certain fundamental rights come with the condition of being human—they come with the skin—and no one, no group, no sovereign, not even the people as sovereign, has the moral, the social, or the political right to deprive any one of us of those rights. Any effort to do so is illegitimate. It was the very purpose of our constitutional system and the Bill of Rights to establish a form of government in which the autonomy and integrity of the individual would predominate over the interests of the state, the collective society—the public. The philosophy is that the state exists for the preservation and advancement of the liberty of the individual, not the other way around.

The people retain ample means to protect themselves from dangerous individuals and groups. But the means must be within the confines of law—law which makes certain rights of the individual ironclad, no matter what the collective temptation may be to violate them. Moreover, the equality principle—won at the cost of a Civil War in which more American lives were lost than in all other wars combined—provides a baseline solution: if the threat is so great that the restrictions to be imposed on liberty are truly necessary and worth the hardships they entail, let them be borne by all, equally, regardless of race. If Arabs are to be questioned and frisked at airports, let us all be questioned and frisked in the same way. Equality has the built-in virtue that, if all are similarly burdened, the public will not tolerate unnecessary and excessive measures.

The Antidemocratic Nature of the Bill of Rights

In late October 2001, six weeks after the terrorist attacks, I attended a presentation by Professor Arthur Miller at the forty-fifth reunion of my Harvard Law School class, in which a television journalist on a panel answered each issue on how to reconcile liberty with security by applying his "MOS" standard: what would the Man on the Street say? Unsurprisingly, on his scorecard, individual rights lost out to collective security every time. The man on the street will almost always say that he believes in civil liberties, "but." "I am all for civil liberties, but," is the argument for racial profiling, the argument always made when rights are asserted in hard cases. People are in favor of the presumption of innocence, but against the pretrial release of suspects; in favor of freedom of speech and assembly, but against allowing Nazis to march in Skokie, Illinois; in favor of freedom of religion, but against permitting a Ku Klux Klan rally around a fiery cross.

The argument that civil liberties and racial equality are good, but not in times like these, reflects an ignorance or lack of faith in the very purpose of the Bill of Rights. The Bill of Rights is by design antidemocratic, intended to restrain reactions to the offensive, the unpopular, and the threatening; intended to stand as a bulwark against popular will when the public is most agitated; intended for stormy times, groups, and people, which is when the rights are most needed. Its purpose is to protect the individual and minorities from a tyrannical majority.

The question of whether the antidemocratic nature of the Bill of Rights is a sound and just concept is addressed in philosopher John Rawls's 1971 work, *A Theory of Justice*. Rawls asks what rights people would vote for if they had to work out such rights and laws under a "veil of ignorance." Under this veil of ignorance, Rawls theorizes, each person would have to decide, in a group vote, on the rights each of them would have, and what steps the collective group might take against each of them, without knowing in advance what his or her status and power would be in the society that would follow and function under these rules.

Thus, each person would have to vote on the rules without knowing whether he or she would, for example, be in a racial, ethnic, or political minority, would be rich or poor, talented or untalented, highly intelligent or not, physically strong or weak, etc.

To protect self-interest, one is thus forced to contemplate such potential vulnerabilities as being in an unpopular minority, or being erroneously accused of a crime, or otherwise being disliked or targeted by the group for punishment, restriction, or other action. Everyone is therefore impelled to gauge the best distribution of power and rights between the group and the individual, looking at it from both points of view. Rawls concludes that a rational person going through this process is most likely to end up where the Founders did, with a set of individual rights approximating those in the Bill of Rights.

The Shoe on the Other Foot: Who Will Be Profiled Next?
Supporters of racial profiling need the Rawls "veil of ignorance" perspective. It is potentially dangerous to many of us to establish the precedent that members of a racial or ethnic minority may be treated differently. Being called out of line at the airport and sent to a separate area with all other members of one's ethnic group is of course not in the same league as being sent to a concentration camp. But surely it is more than the "pretty small imposition" and mere "inconvenience and embarrassment" with which Michael Kinsley dismisses it in his *Washington Post* article.

Consider the atmosphere generated around the lives of an ethnic group that is sorted out in public for special treatment. We are seeing and hearing the anguish of Arab- and Muslim-Americans, sudden pariahs in a hostile atmosphere currently driving some to change their family names. Consider, too, proposals for national identification cards as another security measure; surely, if Arabs are a special category, such cards would prominently identify the bearer's ethnicity. Given racial profiling and a terrorized public subjected to a few more bombings, how far would we be from requiring Arabs to wear yellow crescents, as Jews in Nazi Germany were once made to wear yellow stars?

This is a path we should not follow. It is appalling to contemplate that, after an act of Jewish terrorism in the United States, all young Jews would be specially screened at airports, or that, just because the suspect is white, all white people would be subjected to special screening in cities like Washington, D.C., where they are in the minority. Racial profiling is a dangerous standard, hazardous to us all.

The National Spirit: What Is America?

Americans could benefit from looking at how another society responded when an ethnic group in its midst was targeted. Marcel Ophuls's 1970 documentary film *The Sorrow and the Pity* chronicles the shameful complicity of the French during the German occupation of the 1940s, including their cooperation in rounding up Jews for deportations to death camps. Another documentary film, *Weapons of the Spirit*, tells the story of Le Chambon-sur-Lignon, a small agricultural village in the mountains of Southern France, where 5,000 Jews fleeing the Nazis were taken in and sheltered by 5,000 Christians. This occurred organically, without a plan: Jewish families just started showing up, and the Huguenots of Le Chambon, with a history of persecution and concern for the scapegoat, took them in, one family at a time.

Forty years later, Pierre Sauvage, born in the town in 1944 to Jewish parents hiding there, returned to make the film. He asks villagers, now in their eighties, who had provided refuge, "What made you take in these people? Weren't you putting yourself in danger?" On camera we see an elderly lady shrug self-effacingly and answer, "We were used to it." A former school director explains, "It was the human thing to do." Eventually, the local Vichy prefect and the German army commander became aware of the presence of fugitive Jews, but for some unknown reason, both looked the other way. The Jews of Le Chambon escaped the Holocaust. Sauvage speculates that even the French prefect and the Nazi commander may have been caught up in the contagious goodness of Le Chambon. Bill Moyers, introducing the film, asks us to consider what each of us would have done if this had happened in America.

Of course, the antidemocratic and counterintuitive nature of civil liberties makes them unpopular. Opinion polls usually show that if the question is cast in a controversial context, about two-thirds of the public are opposed to any particular provision of the Bill of Rights. "Eternal vigilance is the price of liberty" is the adopted motto of the American Civil Liberties Union, and eternal vigilance—that is, an awareness by our political leaders, by our teachers, by our public commentators—has been lacking for a long time. The notion prevails that "civil libertarians" are a special interest group, and that civil liberties are an expendable luxury suitable only for calm times. Pierre Sauvage comments near the beginning of *Weapons of the Spirit* that when the crisis of the Nazi occupation came, Le Chambon found that it had the quality of leaders it needed and deserved. Our leaders, pundits, and other sculptors of the culture would do well to revisit the Jefferson Memorial and ponder the great man's warning, engraved on one of the walls: *Can the liberties of a nation be secure when the people have lost the conviction that those liberties are the gift of God?*

The system of civil liberties represents the highest qualities in law and government to which humans can aspire. As the philosopher Martin Buber maintains in his classic work, *I and Thou*, the challenge of being human is to rise above seeing people different from us as "the other," an object, a thing, an "it," and to see them instead as a part of an "I and Thou," a part of our very selves.

The Bill of Rights, civil liberties, and the primacy of the individual over the state are our most valuable heritage, our most unique and exalted national quality. They, more than mountains and free markets and consumerism, are what define our highest character as a people. We have shown in Afghanistan that we can defend our lives with weapons of war. Hopefully we can also preserve what we live for with weapons of the spirit.

RENEWING THE CALL OF *GIDEON*
2003

Originally published in Washington Lawyer, *June 2003, based on an address delivered at the D.C. Superior Court on March 18, 2003, the fortieth anniversary of the decision in* Gideon v. Wainwright.

Gripped by fear, Americans are acquiescing in a historic repeal of basic rights long taken for granted, including the right to counsel. This year, the fortieth anniversary of *Gideon v. Wainwright*, is a good time to remember the decision and get back to basics. In the early 1960s, as an associate in Arnold, Fortas & Porter, I was one of a team that worked with Abe Fortas when he was appointed to represent Clarence Gideon before the Supreme Court.

The *Gideon* case exemplifies the human institution of law at its very best. For this was a case in which a little man, a nobody, asserted his rights and sent a handwritten note from his cell in a penitentiary to the highest court in the land and that court sat up and noticed, appointed an outstanding lawyer to argue the case, and the result was a decision that is a landmark in the history of justice.

The *Gideon* case is about the people in it, the law, and America.

Clarence Earl Gideon was the activist, the man who took action to demand his rights; Abe Fortas was the lawyer appointed to argue Gideon's case in the Supreme Court; and Robert L. McCrary Jr. was the Florida judge who had denied Gideon's request for a lawyer and then sentenced him to five years in prison. These are the people this case was about, and we should look at them and their actions, because ultimately law and justice are what the activists, the lawyers, and the judges make them, for better or for worse.

Gideon was a drifter and a gambler who, at age fifty-one at the time of his trial for burglary in 1961, had served over a dozen different prison sentences. Gideon wrote of himself: "[D]ue to my limited education and also to the utter folly and hopelessness [of] parts of my life . . . I will not be proud of this biography, it will be no cause of pride." But he also wrote: "I have no illusions about law or courts and the people who are involved in them . . . I believe that each era finds a improvement in law[,] each year brings something new for the benefit of mankind. Maybe this will be one of those small steps forward . . ."

Although the man had not made much use of his life, as Anthony Lewis wrote in his book about the case, *Gideon's Trumpet*, "a flame still burned in Clarence Earl Gideon . . . He had not lost his sense of injustice."

The history of justice is in large part the history of people like Gideon, who, downtrodden though they may be, keep their sense of justice and have the spirit and the courage to stand up for themselves and others.

Abe Fortas, in 1962, was one of the best lawyers in the country. He had become wealthy representing big-business clients, but he never lost his sense of justice, and his law firm frequently took cases that stood for principles of liberty, whether or not they got paid for them. In the months after Fortas was appointed to represent Gideon, he put five of us to work on the case. Fortas told us at the outset that our goal was to do more than just win the case: we had to establish a solid legal ruling that would endure.

"We don't just want to win by a 5-to-4 vote of the Supreme Court, or 6-to-3, or 7-to-2," he told us. "We're going to win this case 9-to-0."

We did a ton of research, all of it directed by Fortas, covering every imaginable subject related to the issues, from the position of each Supreme Court justice in every right-to-counsel case that had come to the Court in the last twenty years, to the right to counsel in England, Russia, and each of the fifty states.

Abe Fortas designed the arguments and the structure of the brief; Abe Krash, a young partner, wrote most of it; then we repeatedly honed it. Finally, as Fortas made changes on the third set of galleys, he told us not to bring them to him anymore. "I'll never stop making changes," he said. Fortas was a perfectionist.

Later, as Fortas and I rode in a taxi to the Supreme Court for the oral argument, he had another idea. "When we get to the Court," he said, "go up to the fifth-floor library and find a biography on Clarence Darrow and see whether the greatest criminal defense lawyer of the 1920s was able to defend himself when he was prosecuted on a bribery charge." I rushed up to the library and found that, sure enough, Clarence Darrow had hired another lawyer to represent him at his trial, and when Darrow tried to participate at the beginning of the trial, his knees shook so much he could hardly stand. I wrote a quick note, went down to the courtroom, and handed it to Fortas just before the *Gideon* case was called. In his thirty-minute presentation, Fortas told the Court that even Clarence Darrow needed a lawyer when he was on trial. Months later, the Supreme Court ruled in favor of Gideon's right to counsel, 9-to-0.

Abe Fortas the lawyer, who in 1965 himself became a

Supreme Court justice, teaches us craftsmanship, excellence, devotion, going all the way, leaving nothing undone.

The third and most important category of people essential to make the ideals of law and liberty a reality is the judiciary—not just the nine justices on the Supreme Court, but also the trial and appeals judges in federal and local courts all over America. In the end, the judges are the guardians of the Constitution; they are the ones who determine whether we are a free people who truly enjoy the civil liberties promised in the Constitution and for which this country stands.

When Clarence Gideon appeared before him in 1961 and said, "I am innocent, I am penniless, I need a lawyer," Florida judge Robert McCrary turned him down. The judge said that under Florida law, lawyers were appointed only in death penalty cases. It was true that Florida law required counsel only in death cases, but the judge did not mention that the state also allowed judges to appoint counsel in other cases, like Gideon's. Instead of seeing the vital principles of fairness that were at stake, Judge McCrary just went along with the prevailing attitudes. In this way, he did not live up to the highest calling of being a judge; he did not fulfill the highest purpose of law.

That purpose is to give the little person, the powerless person, a chance to stand up against a powerful institution, whether it be the government or a corporation.

Walter Van Tilburg Clark, in his book *The Ox-Bow Incident*, wrote:

True law, the code of justice, the essence of our sensations of right and wrong, is the conscience of society . . . None of man's temples, none of his religions, none of his weapons, his tools, his arts, his sciences, nothing else he has grown to, is so great a

thing as his justice, his sense of justice. The true law . . . is the
spirit of the moral nature of man . . .

When we enter the court, we enter the temple of justice. And that's why the *Gideon* case is so important. For the right to counsel is the most important of all rights, because without it none of the other rights can be protected. In this sense, the right to counsel is the key to the temple of justice.

It is tragic that today the right to counsel is under attack by the federal government as never before. The question is whether at this time of fear and war we will abandon the traditional rights that define us as a people.

In the less than two years since the terrorist attacks of September 11, 2001, the Bush administration has vastly expanded government powers at the expense of traditional rights. Worst of all, the right to counsel has been seriously undermined in a number of ways. For one, the government claims the power to hold anyone it thinks is an "enemy combatant" for as long as it wants, without charging that person with a crime, without giving him a day in court, without allowing him to see a lawyer. Two American citizens are now being held that way, and one of them was arrested in Chicago, so the government has stretched the term "enemy combatant" far beyond a soldier captured on the battlefield.

Indeed, the rollback of civil liberties is extending beyond the bounds of terrorism. For example, in the case of John Lee Malvo, the seventeen-year-old Jamaican accused of being the beltway sniper, the federal government ordered the man transferred from Maryland, where an attorney had been appointed to represent him, to Virginia, where there is a better chance of getting a death sentence.

The authorities then maintained that, during the transfer, Maryland no longer had jurisdiction, the Maryland lawyer therefore no longer represented Malvo, so there was no defense lawyer until Virginia appointed a new one. In the interim the authorities physically prevented the Maryland attorney, as well as a court-appointed guardian, from getting to Malvo, induced the boy to sign a waiver of his right to counsel, and extracted from him a confession.

This manipulative, jurisdiction-shopping subterfuge is a betrayal of the right to counsel and the rule of law.

History also teaches us the unreliability of confessions obtained by intimidation and deceit. Let's look at one more case, that of Abdallah Higazy, a thirty-year-old Egyptian arrested by the FBI at the Millennium Hilton Hotel in New York soon after the terrorist attacks destroyed the World Trade Center. The hotel had reported to the FBI that just after the attacks hotel staff found in Higazi's room, which looked out onto the World Trade Center, a transceiver, which is a radio device for communicating from the ground to airplanes overhead. Higazi, a graduate student at Brooklyn Polytechnic College who had also served in the Egyptian air force, repeatedly denied that he had ever seen the transceiver. Finally, under FBI interrogation, without a lawyer to counsel him, Higazi, while still denying any involvement in the attacks, confessed that the transceiver was his. The FBI charged Higazi with lying in an investigation. A day or so later an airplane pilot came to the hotel to claim the transceiver—it was not Higazi's after all. The hotel employees had been mistaken in saying they had found it in his room. The government dropped the charges, and Higazi, after a month in jail, was released.

Why did he confess to something that was not true? He said it was because the FBI had threatened to have members of his family arrested. The FBI denied this and said that they had merely told him that if he didn't admit to owning the transceiver, he would not be able to continue his schooling in Brooklyn. So by the FBI's own admission, they got the false confession by intimidating Higazi.

The great principle of the *Gideon* case is in danger today. A frightened nation hunkers down and begins cutting corners on the rule of law and on civil liberties. We need to remind ourselves what we are about as a nation, a society, a people.

It was the purpose of our constitutional system and the Bill of Rights to establish a form of government in which the liberty of the individual would be a higher priority than the interests of the government, of the collective society, of the public. The philosophy is that each individual does not exist for the protection of government, but that government exists for the protection of individual liberty.

The government still has ample means to protect the public from dangerous individuals and groups. But the means must be within the rule of law, law that makes certain rights of the individual ironclad, no matter what the collective temptation to violate them.

The argument that we can't afford civil liberties in times like these is wrong. The Bill of Rights is by design antidemocratic, intended to restrain the public's reactions to the offensive, the unpopular, and the threatening; intended to stand as an iron wall of protection against popular will when the public is most upset; intended for harsh times, groups, and people, which is when the rights are really needed.

The purpose of the Bill of Rights is to protect the individual and minorities from an aroused and tyrannical majority.

As the country passes through a hard time and abandons its commitment to civil liberties, what can be done, what can make a difference? We need activists like Clarence Earl Gideon, who speak out for the rights of themselves and others. We need first-class lawyers, like Abe Fortas, to fight for those rights.

Most of all, we need our judges to be strong and courageous, and not simply to go along with the prevailing currents, as did Judge McCrary in 1961 when he refused to give Gideon a lawyer, as did the Supreme Court in 1944 when it approved sending 120,000 Japanese Americans into concentration camps. As do judges all too often in times of war or crisis.

Today we need our judges to stand against the tide, as did those few courageous Southern judges who stood against racial segregation in the 1960s: Frank Johnson in Alabama, Bryan Simpson in Florida, Skelly Wright in Louisiana. We need judges to follow *those* role models, to maintain their independence from the executive branch and from public passions and fears, and to challenge the arguments that protection from terrorists or beltway snipers requires us to sacrifice the right to counsel and other basic liberties.

SHORT-TIMER'S STROLL
2003

On Friday of this week, Good Friday, Lester "LT" Irby is going home. We've known this was going to happen since December 10. But there's many a slip between cup and lip. LT and I had put out our very best at the parole hearing in that dingy little room in the federal prison at Terre Haute, Indiana, the penitentiary that has the only federal execution chamber, the one where they lethally injected Timothy McVeigh. We felt we had done well, and knew it when, as we left the room, the guard Kevin Beaver whispered to us, "Good job."

Fifteen minutes later, the hearing officer called us back in and gave us the good news. He was recommending parole effective April 20. It took another month and we breathed another sigh of relief when we got word that the United States Parole Commission had approved the parole. We weren't home safe, though. Prison is a dangerous place, and much of the danger is in the accidental malice of the institution. Three times in the last four years, as LT and I struggled with repeated denials of parole, he narrowly missed the bullet of false disciplinary charges that would have assured he would never get out. The last one was a year ago, when he was falsely accused by a guard of trying to instigate a prison riot. We escaped the life sentence that would have resulted when Heaven gave us that rarest of all jewels in the prison system—an honest guard who was willing to break rank and tell the truth—that the guard who accused LT was lying to cover up for his own blunders that caused an incident.

But now these last four and a half hazardous months have passed without incident, and LT will be released in just three days. The feds arranged a forty-eight-hour bus trip, complete with several five- to ten-hour waits in terminals to transport him from Terre Haute to Newark. Fortunately, LT's sister Bobbie has a friend with an airline and was able to get him a $50 ticket to fly home. The guard Kevin Beaver offered to use his day off to drive LT to the airport in Indianapolis.

Now Irby and I are on the phone, glowing.

"The other inmates here are counting it down with me," he says. "One guy says to me, *Seven and a wake-up.* Next day another guy says, *Six and a wake-up.* Just now a guy says to me, *Hey, LT, two and a half and a wake-up.* Man, I tell you."

"Give me your schedule," I say, "I want to be with you the whole day."

His sister's airline friend, Erol, will meet him at the plane and take him to the right spot in the airport to connect with Bobbie and her thirty-year-old son Oji, with whom LT will live until he gets a job and a place of his own. He needs the escort because LT went to prison for armed robbery at the age of twenty-six in 1973, has been in for thirty years, and is now being released at age fifty-six into a world he doesn't know.

"My sister sent me clothes and they all fit except the shirt which was a little too big. This morning I was putting on the necktie and I got this whole flood of memory, the first time I ever put on a necktie. I haven't put on a necktie since I been in, but I got the knot perfect first time; it all came back to me."

"You're ready, LT," I say, "you'll slip in like a hand into a glove."

"Yeah, I'm ready. Only, last night I was tossing and turning. The anticipation. I always sleep good, but last night, I couldn't sleep, just tossing and turning. But good tossing and turning, feeling good. Man, I feel good."

"Will you and Bobbie and Oji go from the airport out somewhere, or straight home?"

"We probably stop and see Bobbie's older son Ricky and his wife, then to Bobbie's house to get with my mother. Probably Ricky and his wife will come too, and some of my mother's friends will be there."

"Oh," I say, "they've got a gathering to welcome you."

"I think so. They don't say, but I think so."

"Good Friday," I say, "and Resurrection."

"Yeah."

"If you get a chance, LT, call me. But not if it's too much, with all that feeling, and you'll be tired."

"Oh, man, you are definitely on the agenda, I'll call for sure."

"If you feel like it," I say, "keep a little journal, a diary, these are special days."

"I been thinking about that," he responds. "I been thinking about writing something about it, and calling it 'Seven and a Wake-Up.'"

"Yes, just right."

"Well, I'm gonna get going now," he says. "Take me a stroll outside in the sun. It's eighty-six degrees here and the sun will feel good. Take me a short-timer's stroll. That's what they call it. All these years I been saying to guys, *Enjoy your short-timer's stroll.* Now I get to do my short-timer's stroll."

A TALE OF THREE TAXIS
2003

It was the best of times, it was the worst of times—fall in New York and Bush in Washington. "Namaste" is Hindu for "the Spirit in me greets the Spirit in you." That's what my daughter Kathy said when I asked her to guess the parting words of the Indian driver when he left me at Newark Airport. A good guess, but wrong. His last words to me as his cab pulled away were a loud "Fuck you."

He had picked me up at Hofstra Law School in Hempstead on Long Island at the conclusion of a three-day symposium on judges' ethics organized by my friend Monroe Freedman. Discussing with scholars and judges all the things that judges do wrong is my idea of a good time.

We had started the two-hour journey genially enough at just after three p.m. on a pleasant Tuesday afternoon, September 16, with plenty of time to make my six-fifteen flight back to Oregon. He seemed polite, mild-mannered. But the first time we hit a traffic jam, he began to mutter and fidget with growing agitation. After five minutes of this, as I felt my stomach begin to tighten, I mentally lowered the tip I was planning to give him on this $85 taxi ride from $15 to $10. Some time after we were back in the flow of traffic, I became aware that my throat was stinging in reaction to cigarette smoke. It took me several minutes to realize that the fumes were coming not from outside the cab, but from the cigarette that he was surreptitiously smoking. I asked him to put it out and he courteously responded, "No problem, sir." Good enough. Nevertheless, his $10 tip was wavering.

We got to the airport at 4:45, having made excellent time. Now the troubles began. He couldn't find the United Airlines terminal, and I must say Newark Airport seems to have been designed and signed to extract information from terrorist suspects. My Indian driver was no longer mild-mannered, but had worked himself into a fit, now loudly cursing. At one point, he accidentally left the airport and we found ourselves on a speedway heading into Newark. Now I became concerned at his glum and brooding silence. It felt as if he had passed through the several stages of grieving and was sinking into a resigned depression. I could not afford for him to resign, so after awhile, I asked him, "What's your plan?" He scowled at me, and did a sudden and illegal U-turn, which, to my great relief, headed us back toward the airport.

At last we pulled up to the United terminal that had eluded us for thirty minutes. It was five-fifteen, and I still had an hour to grab a bite and catch my plane. Just the same, his tip had dropped to $5. At least, until he handed me the credit card slip to sign. As I looked at the $85 charge and began mentally to vacillate between a tip of $5 and $10, he said, "The gratuity is twenty percent, sir."

"Twenty percent? Who says so?"

"That's the rule," he said.

"There's no rule," I snapped.

Getting out of the cab, I grabbed my bags, signed the slip, and handed it to him.

"Why is there no gratuity on here?" he demanded, not at all mild-mannered.

"Because of the way you've behaved," I responded.

He took his leave with a parting greeting not even close to "Namaste."

The taxi ride before that one had been better. I'd come into the Hempstead station on the Long Island Rail Road on Sunday, a forty-minute ride from Brooklyn where I'd spent the week with my son Johnny and his wife Kara at their brownstone in the pleasant multiethnic Fort Greene neighborhood. The old black guy sitting in his beat-up taxi in front of the station had beckoned me into the front seat. Sitting in the back was a matronly black woman and her little girl, all gussied up for church. We dropped his passengers off at the church as I restrained myself from kissing them goodbye. Then he and I started into a chorus of happily bashing the stupidity and thuggishness of Bush and the insanity of the invasion of Iraq. As we pulled into Hofstra University, however, he slid over into the subject of the Middle East.

"Look what they done to them poor Palestinians," he said. "All they want is a place of their own, and they won't let them be."

Well, I thought, *it's more complicated than that.*

"I mean, think how you'd feel," he continued, "if someone come in and pushed you off your place, and you say, *Hey, man, what you do that for?* and they say, *G-d give us this land.*"

A good point, but still oversimplified. I decided that there was not enough time to get into it—the Hofstra symposium was about to begin, and this guy and I had been enjoying each other too much to spoil it at the parting. We bade each other a happy goodbye.

The point the old driver made had in fact been stuck in my face a week earlier, on the first of my three taxi adventures.

My flight from Medford, Oregon through San Francisco had gotten into Newark airport on Saturday night, September 6, about 11:15 p.m. At 11:45 I got in a taxi driven by an Arab, a Palestinian I guessed, because his eyes resembled those of Yasser Arafat. We made good time, getting to the Manhattan Bridge in lower Manhattan in just thirty minutes. It was 12:15 a.m., just ten minutes away from Johnny and Kara's house. But the traffic on the bridge was impossible. It took us an hour and ten minutes of bumper-to-bumper inching along to cross that forsaken bridge, and I didn't get to the house until 1:30 a.m.

The ordeal brought back the memory of the summer of 1955 when, between my second and third years of law school, I was living with my friend Phil's grandmother in Brooklyn and working in a soda bottling factory in Queens. In the morning, trying to get to Queens, I'd taken a wrong turn and found myself heading toward the Manhattan Bridge into Manhattan. I was embedded in traffic and could not back out. So I had to wait out the slow-moving traffic, wasting fifteen minutes getting across the bridge, then navigating through the streets to return back over the bridge into Brooklyn so I could pick up my route to the factory in Queens. I arrived to work thirty minutes late and got chewed out for it. Coming home that evening, exhausted, I was moving along when suddenly I found I'd made a wrong turn and was again heading over the hated Manhattan Bridge. It was summer, hot, no air-conditioned cars then. I calmly rolled up all the windows in my car, and cursed and screamed all the way over the bridge and part of the way back.

You can understand then why I felt compassion for my Palestinian driver when after fifteen minutes of our grinding wait on the Manhattan Bridge, he started to scream and curse. Mentally, the $5 tip I'd planned on the $50 fare increased to $10. I thought to say something to mollify him, maybe distract him by asking about his wife and children. My intuition vetoed the proposal, however, and I sat suffering in silence.

By the time thirty-five minutes had passed and we were only halfway across the damned bridge, he saw that the traffic was just as bad going back the other way, and grumbled that he would earn no more fares that night—New Jersey taxis can't pick up passengers in New York—and that he wouldn't get home to bed until five a.m. The tip went up to $15.

When it seemed like it couldn't get any worse, something awful happened. He paused a moment too long as the traffic at last moved a car's length, and a huge white van in the other lane slipped in ahead of us. When you're stuck in traffic like that, every inch gained seems to take a lifetime, so a vehicle getting in ahead of you feels like a theft of your land. Worse yet: this van had Connecticut license plates and slogans all over it. The slogans were all in Hebrew, except one in English which asserted: *The Land of Israel Is God's Gift to the Jews.*

Blessedly, the Palestinian's rantings did not change in content. When he finally left me at the house, I didn't even mind that he didn't thank me for the $20 tip.

WIN SOME, LOSE SOME
2004

The young white man and the black woman were screaming at each other in front of the polling station. I asked her to step to one side with me and tell me what the argument was about. The young man, like me, was a lawyer poll-watcher; he was there for Bush, I for Kerry. He strode over as he heard what she was telling me, shouting that she was lying.

"Whoa, who asked you?" I shouted back.

"I'm not going to stand for her telling lies!" he yelled.

Let's see, I thought, *my Volunteer Poll-Watchers for Kerry instructions were: wear a dark blue suit, a blue shirt, and a blue tie; be assertive and firm, but not overly aggressive.*

"You're not going to stand here at all!" I yelled back. "Butt out. Get out of here. This is a private conversation."

He walked away, and I got the story from Linda, a very aggressive Democratic Party organizer. Then I sat down with the Republican, Ryan Nelson, a volunteer from the prestigious Washington, D.C. law firm, Sidley Austin, and nailed down the legal points in issue. He was arguing that Linda and her team, there to offer help to disabled and elderly people who might need assistance at the voting machines, had no right to be inside the polling station, and had to remain fifty feet away from the doorway to the polls. An election official mediated the conflict between Nelson and me, ruling that those offering to help voters could not be inside the polling station, but since they were merely assisting, not campaigning, they could be right outside the door, not fifty feet away.

Nelson and I had a couple more encounters over the next few hours. When I was leaving at the end of my four-hour gig, I walked over to him and said, "See that woman?" pointing to Ann, who'd just come into the room. "That's my wife. I'm leaving now and she's relieving me. She's a real pushover, Ryan, so now you can get away with whatever you want." We parted laughing.

The whole two weeks of poll-watching went like that. Nothing momentous. Just skirmishing with the opposition and election officials. Some of the officials were cooperative and gracious when we brought irregularities to their attention, while others were defensive and belligerent, like the two who threatened to have me removed from their polling stations.

In my imagination, my family and I had parachuted into Miami, behind enemy lines, three weeks before the election of November 2, 2004. The kids went to work canvassing neighborhoods, driving elderly voters to the polls, and campaigning. Ann and I spent our first week working for the organizers of the Miami-Dade County Volunteer Poll-Watchers for Kerry. We phoned the list of 430 volunteer lawyers, prompting them to turn in their enrollment forms, come to two-hour training sessions, and study their forty-page poll-watchers manuals.

Florida has early voting, so for two weeks before Election Day, Ann and I had poll-watching assignments at various public schools and libraries. With both Republican and Democratic lawyers watching them, election officials pretty much did a good job.

My only clear contribution had nothing to do with the voting. On Monday, November 1, I'd gone down to the Miami Beach Traffic Department at 12th and Washington Avenue to get my parking card renewed. The machine that issues and renews parking cards had an *Out of Order* sign on it, and there were twelve people in line, being attended by two slow-functioning window clerks. I had to wait an hour, and by the time I got helped, there were thirty people in line behind me.

As my number was called, the clerk at the other window put up a *Closed* sign and left. I said to the woman helping me, "Where's she going? She can't close the window, there are thirty people in line and it's taking too long."

The woman, continuing to process my card, shrugged and said, "She's gone to lunch."

"At ten o'clock in the morning?" I called through the glass window at a woman working at a desk. "Come to the window!" I yelled. "Get off the computer. There's a long line. Help these people!"

The computer woman briefly turned to scowl at me while continuing her work.

I began banging my fist on the glass window and shouting, "Get someone at this window, there's a long line here, get someone at this window!"

A supervisor-type appeared at the window. "Is there a problem, sir?" she asked politely.

"Yes," I said. "This window can't be closed, the line is too long. And what's being done about that machine that's out of order?"

"Its all being attended to, sir," she said, walking away.

"Attending is not good enough!" I shouted, banging loudly on the window again. "Open this window!"

Another clerk came and opened the window.

Kerry lost the election, but I hope the traffic office changed for good.

THE CREED OF A LIBERAL
2005

An earlier version of this essay was published in
Proud to Be Liberal *(Ig Publishing, 2006)*

L iberalism pursues fairness, justice, and equality for all, and the maximum individual liberty.

Liberals Accept Life's Challenge of Paradox

This is no simple task. Equality is an essential element of fairness and justice, yet equality is incompatible with liberty. If everyone is completely free, the strong will prosper and the weak will suffer. British economist and philosopher E.F. Schumacher noted that it was brilliant of the French, in their revolutionary slogan, to place between the opposites of "Liberty" and "Equality" the human virtue that reconciles them, "Fraternity"—that is, brotherhood.

So to be a liberal, one must be able to live and cope with paradox, one must embrace "fraternity," the oneness of all people. To be a liberal is to strive to master the essential ironies of all life. The most universal and fundamental of life's paradoxes are life vs. death, growth vs. decay, change vs. stability. From these come the great social and political paradox of liberty vs. order that underlies the choices in all social structures. It is a major virtue of the liberal that she struggles with this paradox rather than opting for one-sided resolutions that sacrifice one or the other.

A dramatic example of the liberal coping with this paradox is the American Civil Liberties Union's unwavering defense of freedom of speech, even for American Nazis and the Ku Klux Klan. Intrepid scholarly efforts have shown that it is impossible to construct a law which would ban the speech of these loathsome groups without undermining the free speech protections of all other dissident groups. For if the government is given the power to suppress their speech, no one's right of free speech is safe. It is why liberals, including priests and rabbis, who are fervent in their faith, nevertheless fight to keep religion out of the public schools. Ask a Christian fundamentalist if he wants prayer in the public school if he is living in a Muslim-majority town and the prayer is likely to be addressed to Allah while facing Mecca.

The paradox came home to me in 1978, at the Jewish Community Center in Cleveland, where I was defending the ACLU's representation of the Nazis. It was a bitter pill to be confronted by Holocaust survivors in the audience, while outside teenage Jewish pickets carried signs saying, *Jews Who Defend Nazis Are an Abomination.*

Despite the unpopularity of the ACLU's position with the public, these cases are never hard ones for the courts—which see quite clearly the nature of the problem, and invariably rule in favor of the free speech rights of the Nazis and Klan. But the ACLU pays dearly for its stance. In 1978, the organization lost a quarter of its membership and funding when it fought for and won the right of the Nazis to march in Skokie, Illinois.

The ACLU's action in Skokie made me proud to be a liberal.

The Three Core Beliefs of Liberals

These are three basic beliefs that define the American liberal, and which are inherent in the liberal position on any issue: 1) that the collective society guarantees every individual the right to safety and the right to work, subsistence, education, and health care; 2) that the individual does not exist for the protection of the state, rather the state exists for the protection of individual liberty; and 3) that some individual rights are so intrinsic that they may not be abridged, even if the majority of the people feel it necessary for the public interest.

The first principle is set forth in the opening lines of the Constitution:

We the People of the United States, in Order to form a more perfect Union, establish Justice, insure domestic Tranquillity, provide for the common defense, promote the general Welfare, and secure the Blessings of Liberty to ourselves and our Posterity, do ordain and establish this Constitution for the United States of America.

The second principle is fundamental to the concept of America. It was the very purpose of our constitutional system and the Bill of Rights to establish a form of government in which the autonomy and integrity of the individual would predominate over the interests of the state, the collective society—the public. The philosophy is that the state exists for the preservation and advancement of the liberty of the individual, not the other way around.

The third principle is found in the opening lines of the Declaration of Independence:

We hold these truths to be self-evident, that all men are created equal, that they are endowed by their Creator with certain unalienable rights, that among these are Life, Liberty and the pursuit of Happiness.

You don't have to believe in G-d to appreciate that the phrase "endowed by their Creator" means that some rights are so basic, so axiomatic, that they are inherent in the human condition, and that no person, group, or cause can justify their abridgment. This belief is inherent to the liberal creed.

In sum, the liberal's core beliefs are essentially American, deeply embedded our country's founding philosophy and character. To be a liberal is to be committed to what makes America unique in history and in the world—to what we as a people stand for.

The Golden Rule

The most profound virtue of liberalism, however, is the transcendent tenet from which the three core liberal beliefs derive: the Golden Rule—*Do Unto Others As You Would Have Others Do Unto You.* Liberals believe that the Golden Rule should be the dominant social, political, and economic doctrine of any society, and it is the principle that is at the foundation of Rawls's *A Theory of Justice.* This powerful canon is not exclusive to or even original with Christians, but is universal and ageless, found in nearly identical language in almost all traditions, e.g., to name just a dozen: Jewish (Hillel, 50 BC), Greek (Isocrates, 335 BC), Plato and Aristotle (fourth century BC), Thales (fifth century BC), Confucius (500 BC), Pittacus (650 BC), Hindu (the Mahabharata, 1000 BC), and Muslim, Buddhist, Roman, Persian, and Native American.

It is ironic that conservatives in general and the Christian right in particular claim the moral high ground, when so often their political, social, and economic positions are the antitheses of this universal gospel. Liberals believe that what it takes to make the right cut between the collective good on the one hand and individual political and economic freedom on the other is brotherhood—the Golden Rule. That concept is at the heart of liberalism.

I am proud to be a liberal.

WILLOW WIND'S "OZ"—A STINK BOMB

Review by Grandpa Ralph

May 24, 2006

Willow Wind Elementary School's production of *The Wizard of Oz* was, to borrow a phrase from Pauline Kael's review of the movie *Song of Norway*, "of an unbelievable badness." It would be unfair to the word "amateurish" to so characterize this fiasco. Eight- and nine-year-olds could have done a better job.

Peli Norris's Dorothy gave the worst rendition of "Somewhere Over the Rainbow" that this reviewer has ever heard. And, although Dorothy lubricated his joints, the caricaturish stiffness with which Josh Tillman's Tin Man—and Dorothy herself—gawped around the stage suggests they might just as well have saved the oil.

The absurd "sets" consisted of large sheets of brown wrapping paper covered with childlike scrawls or wads of colored paper. Only one—that of the Land of Oz—succeeded, and it did that spectacularly, with large green-ish spires and other simulations of that magical land in the sky. The costumes were adequate—especially that of Toto—but only that of the Cowardly Lion made one feel the presence of the real character. Kudos to Cinda Weatherby, Jasper's mom, for getting it right.

There were some good performances—Julian's juggler, Piat's Wizard, and Ruthie Ferris's Toto—plus the real dog in the audience who actually barked on cue. Otherwise, except for two truly extraordinary performances, this abomination would qualify as a crime against humanity. The two performances that might justify keeping the show's producer and director, drama teacher Cathy Ruel, out of prison were by Grace Powell's prancing Munchkin and Jasper Weatherby's Cowardly Lion. Ms. Powell radiated feminine grace and beauty, seemingly floating in air as she sang and danced. Mr. Weatherby's Lion surpassed that of Bert Lahr in the original, lending the role a combination of exhilarating hilarity and heart-crushing pathos. His energy and dramatic zest seemed barely contained, as if the viewer was on the verge of experiencing every comedy and every tragedy that has ever been staged. Simultaneously, Mr. Weatherby filled in the yawning chasm left by Cathy Ruel's criminally absent direction and prompting, as he pushed and pulled the rest of the cast into their proper positions and choreography, and, *sotto voce*, fed them their cues and sometimes their entire passages.

In sum this calamity was a theatrical *Titanic*, with the exception of my grandchildren, Japer and Grace, who have ahead of them brilliant careers under the lights.

ONCE MORE INTO THE LABYRINTH
2006

L T and I are on the phone, once again struggling with the incompetence that is the Bureau of Prisons. He should have been released from prison into a half-way house in Washington, D.C. on October 6—but it is now November 2 and he's still in prison. My perennial prisoner-client, who in 2003 I sprung from the federal penitentiary in Terre Haute, Indiana, after he'd spent thirty years behind bars for a 1973 armed robbery in which he'd slightly wounded the victim, is now back in for the second time on parole violations. But for more than thirty years now, Lester T-for-Trouble Irby has been an institution in, if not an adopted member of, my family.

The release came on April 18, 2003, when Irby was fifty-six. On Christmas night 2003, Irby, living in East Orange, New Jersey, in a drunken rage, threatened his girlfriend, fifty-five-year-old Mary Frances, with a knife. As she told me, "He's gentle as a lamb, Ralph, I knew he wouldn't hurt me, but I wasn't going to stand for that stuff"—so she called the cops. With Mary Frances's help, the criminal charges were dropped, but the Parole Commission imprisoned LT for another sixteen months for parole violation. In doing so, the Commission disregarded Mary Frances and my pleas to put him in an in-house addiction program we'd lined up for him in Newark.

When they released him into a halfway house in March 2005, it was in Washington, D.C., thus ensuring the final break-up of his relationship with Mary Frances, a civil servant and grandmother of a family that loved LT and had taken him to its heart.

LT began the Salvation Army rehab program and was doing well, but one day wandered off campus and slid back into the drug-and-alcohol groove. In the meantime, my son Johnny had published the collection of short stories *D.C. Noir*, in which was included LT's extraordinary story "God Don't Like Ugly." Johnny arranged for LT, along with George Pelecanos and Laura Lippman, a couple of best-selling crime-fiction authors, to appear before an audience of two hundred intellectuals at a reading at Washington, D.C.'s most famous bookstore, Politics & Prose. Irby stole the show.

The next night, February 2, 2006, at a party I threw to celebrate Irby's success and the October 14 birth of Arthur Jackson Temple, my son Johnny's first child and my sole descendent, Irby approached me, laughing, and said, "I'm having a beer." This led to an exchange of words, and my limiting him to nonalcoholic beer for the rest of the evening.

But, as his parole officer explained to me several days later when LT got busted, "I couldn't help it, Mr. Temple. This has been going on for months. He's got thirty violations—missed parole appointments, missed drug tests, positive test showing alcohol and cocaine. I should have issued a warrant on him a long time ago. I just couldn't hold off any longer."

So LT got another year in prison, with a release date of February 6, 2007. Bill Waggoner, LT's case manager at Lewisburg Federal Penitentiary in Pennsylvania, put him in for a 120-day early release to a halfway house. But the paperwork has gotten jammed up on someone's desk somewhere in the bureaucracy, so LT and Waggoner and I have been on and off the phone with this thing for the past several weeks.

Finally, Waggoner and I have located the jam-up and are making phone calls to try to move the process along and get Irby into the halfway house. Irby and I are feeling good and enjoying the fact that the St. Louis Cardinals just won the World Series, and that we now have Waggoner, who had been lackadaisical about this until I lit a fire under his ass, really working on the problem.

"LT," I say, "you remember when you were drinking that beer at my party after your book reading?"

"It was a nonalcoholic beer," he responds.

"No. After I caught you, I made you switch to nonalcoholic. But it was a real beer."

"Are you sure?"

"I'm sure," I say. "You know why I mention it now?"

"No. Why?" he says.

I say, "I believe we all have both masculine and feminine aspects. And right now you're seeing my feminine nature."

"What do you mean?" LT asks me.

"You know how once you've fucked up, your old lady never lets you forget it?"

LT laughs. "Yeah, I know," he says, "and I sure fucked up. But what made you think of it now?"

"Because once more you and I are struggling with this horrendous bureaucracy. I'm thinking that, after we get you out, if you go back on drugs or alcohol, I'm going to want to mangle your balls."

We part laughing

The journey is the destination.

PART VI

FACING HEART SURGERY

WRESTLING A BEAR
2009

Originally published in the Ashland Daily Tidings, *February 19, 2009*

On January 29, following an angiogram, the doctor told my wife and me that I need open-heart valve-replacement surgery. Normally, the "risk factor" is only 2 percent, but because of my weak left ventricle muscle—the heart's pump—the risk of death during or soon after surgery is 10 to 15 percent. The surgery is scheduled for February 24.

Once before, we were afraid I might die—in 1999 when I was diagnosed with a tongue cancer, and the risk of dying was 20 to 30 percent. The thing is, the mind doesn't hear the news as the highly favorable chance of a cure—which is what happened with the cancer—but as, *Omigod, there's a 15 percent chance I'll die.*

So a significant aspect of contemplating major surgery is how to manage your mind, how to live through the experience—or, as my wife put it: "What am I called upon to do?" I believe all would agree that the best thing to do is to live the time before the surgery as happily as one can—which includes making your loved ones, friends, and others as happy with your situation as possible.

There is, of course, the series of practical things you have to deal with: Selecting a surgeon, updating your will, talking to your kids. NOT making burial plans. If, like me, you have not yet attended to that, just leave it to your mate and kids—this is not the time to get into that subject.

Plainly, it begins with managing one's fears. As noted in my avoidance of burial plans, I've learned several "dos" and "don'ts." They probably don't apply to everyone—we're all so different. But they'll apply to some, and it's a useful list of decisions.

Another of my "don'ts" is the surgery itself. There are some decisions you have to make, like whether to replace the leaking aortic valve with a mechanical valve that will last forever but requires the patient to take the difficult drug Coumadin for the rest of his life. A pig-tissue valve requires no Coumadin but 20 percent of them start leaking again in fifteen years. At my age, seventy-six, the smart choice is the pig valve (whether or not you are Jewish and even if it isn't kosher).

Apart from what you have to decide, I believe it's a mistake to ask the doctor to describe the surgery. I made the mistake of asking, and found that it does me no good to have those images in my mind.

On the other hand, it is a good idea to talk to your mate—or close friends—about the possibility of dying. Not your kids.

What's the objection to dying? It's not as if my life is incomplete.

I've done everything I needed to do, especially with my wife and children, and my civil liberties work. In the last few years I've gotten to write about the experiences I most wanted to write about, and to publish three essays that most fully express my philosophy of liberty and justice. I've been favored with all the acknowledgment one could hope for, most recently an ACLU award before 400 of my peers in my old hometown, Washington, D.C. I got to work for Thurgood Marshall, talk with Martin Luther King Jr., and attend the inauguration of Barack Obama. As they say, who could ask for anything more?

So why fret over the prospects of dying? It's not the loss of consciousness. In the movie *Hannah and Her Sisters*, Woody Allen's father sums up my feeling: "Why should I worry about dying? Now I'm alive. When I'm dead I won't know it. So what's to worry about?"

The fear, the sadness, the sorrow, the thing that makes me occasionally weep, is the thought of not seeing my wife, children, grandchildren, and loving friends again.

And that's the bear. Letting go. If you believe, as I do, that the purpose of life is to become as good a human being as possible, that means not only expanding the capacity to love, but also learning to let go. I think that's the hardest lesson in life. I'm working on it.

TALKING TO MYSELF
2009

Originally published in the Ashland Daily Tidings, *February 20, 2009*

I n managing oneself through a difficult time, like facing open-heart surgery, one needs to manage the mind's inner dialogue. We're all chattering to ourselves all the time. The key is to change it from a conversation between you and you to a conversation between you and an "other," some conceived source smarter than you.

One doesn't have to believe in G-d to do this. What matters is that one conceives of, imagines, if you like, a source that is wiser than oneself. The very act of will, the act of conceiving or imagining a wiser "other," can create a new and critical reality.

Unguided, my mind may go like this:

"I'm furious," I think.

"You can't let her get away with that," I respond.

"No one should have to put up with that kind of abuse," I tell myself.

Myself answers, "I'll never again agree to [whatever the situation was that gave rise to the argument]."

"That will show her," my mind rants.

"And give her a dose of her own medicine," myself adds.

"Yes," I think, "from now on I'll always [fill in the blank]."

"And tell her you'll never [whatever]," adds myself.

And so on, all the while fueling my anger.

But I've learned I can have a better mental conversation with a wiser "other." For many this can be their intuition, their deeper judgment, their "higher self." For Christians it can be Christ. Jews are accustomed to talking to and even arguing with G-d. Just so its someone other than the usual everyday you, someone deeper, higher, smarter, wiser.

Then my mind works this way:

"I'm furious," I think.

"*That's okay,*" says the Other, "*let the anger flow; let it go.*"

"Am I supposed to let her get away with that?" I ask.

"*Don't worry about it,*" says the Other, "*it's only anger.*"

"Only anger?" I respond. "No one should have to put up with that kind of abuse."

"*That's the anger talking,*" says the Other. "*Don't take it too seriously.*"

"Don't tell me that," I say. "I'm too furious to listen to You now."

"*No you're not.*"

"I'll never agree to [such and such] again; from now on I'll always [so and so]. I'll tell her that. That'll show her. Give her a dose of her own medicine."

"*Not a good idea. You know better than to make decisions when you're angry.*"

"So what am I supposed to do—nothing?"

"*Don't worry about it. Good ideas will come to you when you're no longer angry. In fact, your anger is beginning to subside, isn't it—just from talking with Me?*"

"Yes. But I'm still angry."

"*That's okay. Don't suppress it. Just don't act it out. And don't invest in it. Don't clench your fist around it. Just let it spend itself.*"

And so on.

In my mind's thoughts about the surgery, that can mean a conversation like this:

"I'm scared that I'm going to die."

"You're not going to die. You'll be all right."

"How do I know that's really You, Other, and not just me indulging in wishful thinking?"

"You don't. But give it a try. Take a chance. I've never let you down before, have I?"

"But suppose I die?"

"It's not that bad."

"Never to see Annie and Kathy and Johnny again? And how it will tear them up?"

"They can handle it. Your parents died. You've done fine with it. They are strong, solid, have great lives. They'll be all right, and treasure you the way you treasure your parents and your close ones who died. It is life, and they and you are up to living life and death."

This is good enough for me. Maybe you can do better with it. For believers, knowing they speak with the Divine within, it is most powerful. Indeed, that's what faith is most authentically about. Not G-d as an old man in the sky sitting on a throne. Not the churches, temples, and mosques; not the hymns and liturgies; not the theologies, stories, and myths. But a force of nature, an intelligent Consciousness that is pervasive and within all of us.

Communion with That is true faith.

But it works even if you have no faith. There's no doubt we do better if, instead of letting the mind run wild, we focus on the mental dialogue as a conversation with wisdom. There is a part of every human being, something inside, that's smarter than you and me.

WHISTLING IN THE DARK
2009

Originally published in the Ashland Daily Tidings, *February 21, 2009*

I 'm flat on my back, and Michal, my son-in-law, is giving me a yoga therapy treatment, now working on my legs. "You're so brave," he says.

He's referring to the fact that my January 27 angiogram shows that I have to undergo open-heart surgery.

"Michal," I reply, "I'm not brave. I have no choice."

"I mean, you're handling it well," he says.

"Yes, but that's not so brave. If there was some way of getting out of it, I would. For instance, you know how something like 10,000 children in the world are dying every day from disease, war, starvation, and so on? If G-d said to you, *Michal, you've got this valve-replacement surgery coming up, but I will heal you and spare you the surgery if you let me take one additional child today.* Would you do it?"

"No," Michal answers, "I couldn't agree to that."

"That's what I mean," I say. "You're brave. Me? I'd have to think it over."

"Well," he says, "a child!"

"Okay, let me push it one step further. Suppose G-d said to you that, of the 10,000 children that die every day, He will spare one child if you will agree to lose your balls in an accident."

Michal grimaces. "No," he says, "I don't think I could agree to that."

"Me neither. Child or no child. Actually, if G-d made me an offer like that, I'd make a counteroffer. *To take my balls, I'd say to G-d, you'll have to agree to end all suffering by everyone in the world, every man, woman, and child, forever.*"

"Yes," Michal agrees. "And the accident taking the balls has to be painless."

"Even more," I say. "No accident—I just wake up in the morning without balls."

"Yes!" says Michal.

"And if G-d countered, and proposed, *For that, I'll only give you one continent free of suffering,* I'd say, *No, for only one continent—Africa—you only take one ball.*"

"Yes," says Michal, "That's a deal."

Now that I think about it, it's a relief that I only have the surgery to deal with.